PUB WALKS
— IN —
The Cotswolds

THIRTY CIRCULAR WALKS
AROUND COTSWOLDS INNS

Nigel Vile

COUNTRYSIDE BOOKS
NEWBURY, BERKSHIRE

COUNTRYSIDE BOOKS
3 Catherine Road
Newbury, Berkshire

ISBN 1 85306 183 2

Publisher's Note

We hope that you obtain considerable enjoyment from this book; great care has been taken in its preparation. However, changes of landlord and actual closures are sadly not uncommon. We are anxious that all details concerning both pubs and walks are kept as up to date as possible, and would therefore welcome information from readers which would be relevant to future editions.

Maps and photographs by the author
Cover illustration by Colin Doggett

Produced through MRM Associates Ltd., Reading
Typeset by Paragon Typesetters, Queensferry, Clwyd
Printed in England

Contents

150
99ₚ
201

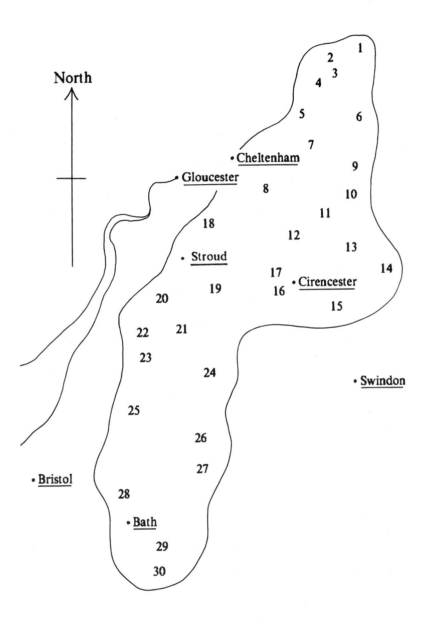

North

Area map showing locations of the walks.

Introduction

A good walk has many ingredients. The landscape is obviously of primary importance – hills, valleys, woodland, and open vistas all linger long in the memory. Man-made attractions also provide a focus of interest, whether it be an ancient church, a ruined abbey or castle, a flight of canal locks or a picturesque village scene. Beyond this, many other factors come into the equation. The absence of noise and traffic matters to some walkers, others dislike road walking, whilst to some a good walk hinges on the presence of interesting companions. A vital consideration at the end of a few hours spent in the 'great outdoors' is the need for refreshment – a welcoming pub or inn that offers both good food and drink. In this book, an attempt has been made to combine as many of these elements as possible.

The Cotswolds provide the fine natural setting for each of these 30 walks. This area of outstanding natural beauty stretches for over 60 miles from Bath northwards to Broadway. The belt of limestone that forms the bedrock of the region lends the area a unique character. It is a fertile landscape of undulating hills crossed by drystone walls, an area of deep woodland and picture-book towns and villages fashioned out of the honey-coloured stone. The architecture of the towns, especially their churches, is the legacy of a flourishing wool trade which brought vast wealth to the area in late medieval times.

The need for refreshment is met by centring each walk on one of the many historic inns that grace the towns and villages of the wolds. It must be said at the outset that this is by no means a definitive selection of Cotswold pubs. Where there was an outstanding walk, the choice of pub was almost incidental. The choice of pubs is also aimed at providing as rich a variety of watering holes as possible. This means that alongside the traditional freehouses and pubs owned by small independent brewers, you will find inns that belong to the somewhat standardised nationwide brewers. A pen portrait of each pub is provided – its history, its character, the food on offer and the range of beers and ales available.

The walks are deliberately low on miles, making them suitable for both the more mature person and a typical family group. Each should provide a morning or an afternoon of exercise and interest, which can be followed by a relaxing meal and a drink in the relevant pub. Whilst the directions and maps in the book are adequate for route-finding, I always feel that walking without an OS map is somehow an incomplete exercise. With this in mind, the appropriate OS Landranger Sheet is specified for each walk, and should be as much a part of your equipment as the obligatory waterproof clothing and stout footwear. Compasses, however, you could dispense with in this part of the world!

A few practical notes. Pub opening hours are the subject of constant change and variation, depending upon demand, seasonal factors and occasionally the whim of the landlord! Generally speaking, all pubs should be open at lunchtimes between 11.30 and 2.30 with food being available between 12 and 2. Equally, in the evenings you can expect the opening hours to extend from 6 until 10.30 with food available from around 7 pm. Rather than specify opening hours in each case, only to be proven wrong by the time the book goes into print, I have given each pub's telephone number if you should wish to make a precise enquiry. Most pubs nowadays display their opening hours at their main entrance, enabling this information to be obtained before you set off on your walk.

The question of parking is a difficult one. If you are doing a walk and not visiting the pub, then you have no right to use the patrons car park. If you intend to visit the pub following the walk, then it is only common courtesy to seek the landlord's permission prior to leaving your vehicle in his empty car park at 9.30 in the morning! On most occasions, landlords are only too happy to oblige. Whatever the circumstances, in most cases I have indicated alternative parking arrangements in the vicinity of the relevant public house.

Don't forget that pubs were not built just for walkers and ramblers. At the end of your walk, you could well be hot and sticky, damp and muddy! It is only polite to both the landlord and his other customers if you attempt some form of wash and brush-up at the end of the walk. If nothing else, at least leave muddy walking boots in your car.

In conclusion, I hope that this book will bring many hours of pleasure for the reader. Not only do these walks open up one of the most pleasant and traditional areas of Britain, they also introduce some of our finest inns and public houses. In my research, I have been pleasantly surprised at the high quality of food that public houses now have on offer. The range of real ales and beers that now enjoy widespread availability was equally surprising. For this, a great debt is due to the pressures exerted by CAMRA. It remains for me to wish you many hours of happy walking.

Nigel A. Vile
Spring 1992

Chipping Campden
The Volunteer

The Volunteer, a traditional Cotswold stone pub, fronts onto the pavement in the Lower High Street of Chipping Campden. It is located away from the centre of the town, literally at the start of the Cotswold Way, and as such is a more appropriate watering hole for walkers than other, perhaps more famous, local inns. The cosy lounge and public bars adjoin a stone courtyard that leads to the beer garden. Unlike most beer gardens, which are simply lawns and picnic tables, this is an example of the old fashioned cottage garden. In the summer, the borders are full of fine old English flowers – hollyhocks, delphiniums, lupins and pansies are everywhere. The pub takes its name from the many local heroes who have over the years been prepared to offer their lives in the service of God, Queen and Country. Reflecting this, the lounge bar contains a small display of wartime memorabilia that includes a selection of servicemen's helmets and berets.

The Volunteer offers a good range of bar food that includes starters, sandwiches, ploughman's lunches, grills, fish dishes and sweets. The Double Gloucester ploughman's has a certain local relevance, whilst the turkey, pork and apricot pie has an irresistible appeal. Other tempting meals that might catch your eye are the mushroom and broccoli quiche, the lemon sole and the home-made steak and kidney pie. The range of sweets is perhaps the best part of the menu! Bread and butter pudding, apple strudel, gooseberry strudel, chocolate fudge cake, apricot crumble and raspberry pavlova present a bewildering choice. The Volunteer is a freehouse where an interesting selection of beers and ales is available. As well as a guest beer, these might typically include Theakston's, Marston's and Flowers.

Telephone: Evesham 840688.

How to get there: Leave the A44 3 miles east of Broadway, and follow the B4081 into Chipping Campden. In the centre of the town, rather than turning right into the High Street, turn left along Lower High Street and the Volunteer is just a few yards along on the left-hand side.

Parking: There is free roadside parking outside the Volunteer.

Length of the walk: 2½ miles. Map: OS Landranger 151 Stratford-on-Avon (GR 148389).

Chipping Campden has had so many superlatives applied to it over the years that it is quite difficult knowing where to begin. Most of the experts are agreed that this is the finest of the Cotswold wool towns, a claim that even the citizens of rival towns such as Painswick or Winchcombe would scarce dispute. The Cotswold masons have

9

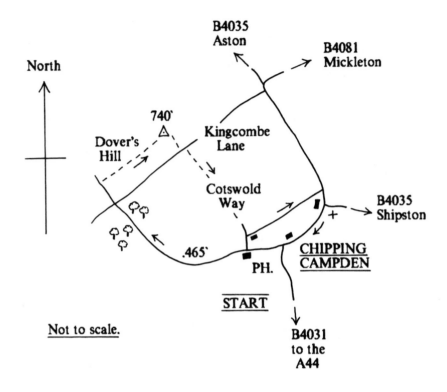

North

B4035
Aston

B4081
Mickleton

740'

Dover's
Hill

Kingcombe
Lane

Cotswold
Way

B4035
Shipston

.465'

CHIPPING
CAMPDEN

PH.

Not to scale.

START

B4031
to the
A44

worked miracles with the local stone, with the result that just about every house in the High Street is worth looking at. The range of styles runs from the Gothic magnificence of Grevel's House to the classical dignity of Bedfont House. The focal point of the High Street is the Market Hall, built in 1627 by Sir Baptist Hicks 'for the sale of cheese, butter and poultry'. Campden church is a fine example of a Cotswold wool church, founded from the wealth of the local woollen merchants. Perpendicular in style, it is dominated by its handsome 15th century pinnacled tower. Above the town lies Dover's Hill, high on the Cotswold scarp, with fine views across the Midland Plain. This was the site of the famous 'Cotswold Olympicks' founded in 1612 by a local lawyer, Robert Dover. The sport included single-stick fighting, the aim of which was to break your opponent's head, as well as shin-kicking! By the mid 19th century, the festivities had degenerated into a mayhem of such violence and drunkenness that they were discontinued, although more recently a milder version of the games has been revived.

   This short walk combines these two elements of Chipping Campden − a gentle climb onto Dover's Hill followed by an exploration of the town itself.

10

The Walk

From the Volunteer, continue away from the town centre along Lower High Street and Park Road to the edge of the town. The road bears to the right before continuing uphill for just over ½ mile to a crossroads at the junction with Kingcombe Lane. Continue straight across and, in just 200 yards, turn right into the Dover's Hill parking area. Head across to the topograph on the edge of the hilltop, which details the many landmarks visible from this fine vantage point. These include the Avon valley, Bredon Hill, the Black Mountains and the Long Mynd in Shropshire. From the topograph, walk north-eastwards along the edge of the hilltop for 600 yards to the triangulation pillar, standing 750 ft above sea level. Over in the right-hand corner of the field, beyond the pillar, a stile leads into the neighbouring field. Follow the edge of this field back down to Kingcombe Lane. Turn left and, in just 50 yards, turn right onto the Cotswold Way. This leads back into Chipping Campden, bringing good views across the town as it descends the hillside.

The path eventually becomes a metalled road – Hoo Lane – that actually leads back to Lower High Street and the Volunteer. Don't go this far yet, however! Where Hoo Lane bears sharply to the right, 200 yards before reaching Lower High Street, turn into the lane on the left-hand side. This is actually called Back Ends, but this name is not signposted. Walk along Back Ends for ½ mile, as it runs parallel to but behind the High Street, before joining the B4081. Turn right, and a glorious prospect awaits you – the final stretch of the walk along Chipping Campden's quite magnificent High Street. There is so much to see – the church, Grevel's House, the Woolstapler's Hall, Bedfont House and the Market Hall being but five examples of the architectural gems that enrich the town. Beyond the Market Hall, continue along Lower High Street and back to the Volunteer.

Broadway
The Horse and Hound

The Horse and Hound inn clearly owes its name to the local hunt, whose hounds are still kennelled in the vicinity. Anti-bloodsport supporters, however, should not assume any contemporary association with the hunt – the link is purely historic! The traditional stone-built inn has somehow managed to maintain an enduring charm, despite the heavy volume of traffic passing within feet of the entrance. Indeed, with its pretty gabled windows, the Horse and Hound still manages to exude a truly rural air.

The lounge and public bars of this Flowers house are dominated by darkwood panelling and furnishings. Window seats, settles and high-backed armchairs accompany a pleasing mixture of circular, square and rectangular tables, whilst several open fires provide welcome warmth for the mid-winter visitor. With its carpeted floors, local photos, country prints, and exposed beams, the Horse and Hound lives up to its claim of being a 'traditional English pub'.

An appetising selection of meals is displayed upon a board inside the bar. Starters might typically include vegetable samosa, prawn cocktail and home-made soup, whilst the main courses provide the visitor with an interesting selection of dishes. Traditionalists might favour steak and kidney pie, Cumberland sausage or gammon, whilst ham and cheese crepe, pork chop and blue cheese, or tuna fish salad, might offer an interesting alternative. Certainly, the portions are substantial and well-garnished, and offer excellent value for money in what can be an expensive corner of the Cotswolds. A decent pint to accompany your meal is provided by both Flowers IPA and Original, although the local Donningtons on offer may tempt you away from the house brews! Telephone: Broadway 852287.

How to get there: Broadway lies on the A44 midway between Moreton-in-Marsh and Evesham. The Horse and Hound inn lies on the northern side of the main street, in the centre of the village.

Parking: There is a car park for patrons to the rear of the Horse and Hound although, given Broadway's popularity as a tourist centre, it is best not to park here whilst spending two to three hours on a walk! There is a public car park just minutes from the inn, on the B4632 (formerly A46) Stratford road. Roadside parking for more than 30 minutes is impossible due to the strict parking regulations in the village.

Length of the walk: 4 miles. Map: OS Landranger 150 Worcester and the Malverns (GR 098375).

Broadway has been described as 'England's best known village', a claim that few would dare dispute. Certainly, the wide main street with its 17th and 18th century houses is a regular coach stop for today's foreign visitors en route to Stratford-on-Avon from London. The neat buildings, with their mullioned windows, gables and stone-slated roofs have been captured by millions of photographers down through the years. It was the earlier coaching traffic back in the 17th and 18th centuries that gave rise to Broadway's original prosperity. The village provided a useful staging point for horse-drawn trade between London and Worcester, with as many as seven coaches passing through each day.

Broadway lies beneath the northern slopes of the Cotswold escarpment, on the edge of the Vale of Evesham. This strenuous circuit climbs onto the hilltops above the village to explore Broadway Hill, whose 1,024 ft summit is the second highest point in the wolds. The views throughout are expansive, and bring ample reward for the 700 ft of climbing involved!

In addition to the natural landscape, the walk passes through Bury End. This small hamlet was the original site of Broadway, and contains St Eadburgha's, the earliest church in the area. St Eadburgha's dates from the Norman period, and is now only used as a place of worship during summer months. The 'new' Victorian church back in Broadway has assumed most of her responsibilities.

13

The Walk

Opposite the Horse and Hound is a footpath signposted 'Recreation Ground. To Old Church 1 mile'. Follow this enclosed path, as it passes between the local recreation ground and a paddock, bordered by an avenue of trees. At the end of the enclosed section, cross a stile and aim for a second stile at the far side of the next field. The path crosses a stream at this point, before following the right-hand field boundary in the next field to a further stile in the corner. Fine views of the surrounding hills provide a pleasing vista, with Broadway Tower featuring prominently on the left-hand hilltop. Continue across the next field to yet another stile, before heading for the red-brick house and the road in the final field.

Turn left on reaching what is the Snowshill road, and walk through the hamlet of Bury End as far as St Eadburgha's church. Bury End was the original village of Broadway, and the church is described locally as 'The Old Church'. St Eadburgha's is Norman in origin, cruciform in layout and has been described as possessing 'a delightfully unspoilt interior which is full of atmosphere'. Certainly, the 'Old Church' at Bury End is architecturally more pleasing than the 'new' Victorian church subsequently established in Broadway itself.

Opposite the church is a footpath signposted to 'Broadway Tower'. Follow this stony track uphill for ¾ mile to a distinct T-junction. Turn right, and in a few yards cross a stile into an open field. The path continues uphill, and passes in front of an isolated bungalow. The views from the front of this bungalow are quite superb, extending across the Vale of Evesham, and taking in the Malvern Hills and nearby Bredon Hill. Continue along the driveway beyond the bungalow and, in 150 yards, turn left in front of a pair of stone gateway pillars. In 300 yards, you will join a lane in front of a farm. Bear left and continue climbing the hill towards the trees at the top. This is truly high wold country, marvellously secluded and open, with traditional sheep farming still very much in evidence.

Almost at the top of the hill, cross a stile on the left-hand side and follow the signposted footpaths for 200 yards through to Broadway Tower. On the way, you will pass Rookery Barn, where snacks and refreshments can be obtained, before passing over a stile on the left-hand side just before an admission kiosk. The kiosk is there because the Tower and surrounding Country Park are private property, with an entrance fee payable. Walkers must therefore stick strictly to the public rights of way through the Park.

Broadway Tower, standing at 1,024 ft above sea level, is a landmark to residents throughout the Severn and Avon valleys. From its castellated roof, the view encompasses 14 counties, and takes in such

14

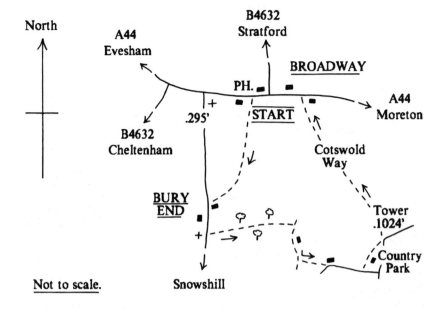

North

A44
Evesham

B4632
Stratford

BROADWAY

PH.

+

.295'

START

A44
Moreton

B4632
Cheltenham

Cotswold
Way

BURY
END

+

Tower
.1024'

Country
Park

Not to scale.

Snowshill

distant landmarks as the Black Mountains and the Berkshire Downs. The story runs that in 1800, the Countess of Coventry was curious to know whether the hill could be seen from her Worcester home. Her husband lit a beacon on the landmark, the answer was in the affirmative, and the immediate order was issued for the tower to be built as a signal station to his residence.

The return to Broadway is by way of the well-signposted Cotswold Way. Below the tower, look for a stile in the left-hand corner of the field. Beyond this stile, follow the right-hand field boundaries downhill towards Broadway, familiar waymarks – white dots on yellow arrows – indicating the right of way. In just over a mile, you will reach Broadway's main street, where a left-turn will return you to the Horse and Hound.

15

Snowshill
The Snowshill Arms

The Snowshill Arms is a picturesque stone-built inn, with a more spacious interior than might be anticipated from the outside. Historically, this would have been a simple village 'local', serving a local community of farmers and shepherds high on the wolds. The views from the rear garden are quite superb, encompassing the valleys and hillsides that lie to the west of the village. Fortunately, the fine outlook can be appreciated from a number of picnic tables, with an excellent play area preventing active and restless youngsters from getting bored! Whilst the views from inside the inn are perhaps not as dramatic, patrons fortunate enough to find a window seat will enjoy a glimpse of some of the village's more attractive buildings.

The Snowshill Arms is a Donnington's house, belonging to a local brewery based in the village of Donnington near Stow. This book also includes Donnington's pubs at Naunton and Stanton, and without doubt these are some of the best inns to be found in the northern wolds. Internally, the Snowshill Arms retains a charm and atmosphere that has not been the victim of modernisation and so-called progress. Quite rightly, there is a wealth of exposed stonework, whilst around the walls hang a selection of local photos and prints. The bar area is furnished with a number of pine tables, whilst an open fire adds to the traditional feel of the inn.

The bar food possesses those two vital qualities looked for by all walkers – ample portions at reasonable prices. The wholesome dishes include home-made soups, ploughman's, gammon steak and fried egg, curries, superb sausages and a selection of salads. Staple pub fare that fits in well with the inn's traditional feel. Meals can, of course, be accompanied by the extremely palatable Donnington BB and SBA brews. In the likely event of your developing a liking for this real beer, supplies can be purchased at the Snowshill Arms to take away with you.

Telephone: Broadway 852653.

How to get there: Snowshill lies 3 miles south of the A44 at Broadway, on an unclassified road leading to Ford. The presence of the NT's Snowshill Manor means that the village is well signposted from its larger neighbour. As you enter the village, the road forks. Bear right, and the Snowshill Arms is a hundred yards along the road on the right-hand side.

Parking: There is a car park for patrons to the rear of the inn. There is also room for careful parking on the road outside the Snowshill Arms.

Length of the walk: 2 miles. Map: OS Landranger 150 Worcester and the Malverns (GR 096336).

Snowshill must rate as one of the most delightful villages in the Cotswolds. The cottages and houses lie tucked into a narrow combe beneath Oat Hill, with scarcely a pair of roof lines on the same level. The motorist finds himself in the same predicament as at Chedworth, one moment looking up to a doorstep, the next down on a chimney! The hub of village life is centred upon the church, whose immediate neighbours include not only the famous Snowshill Manor, but also the local inn.

This is the shortest walk in the book, but I make no apologies for that. By the time that you have explored Snowshill Manor, with its 21 rooms containing Charles Paget Wade's collection of craftsmanship, there won't be that much time left to enjoy a meal at the Snowshill Arms, a visit to the local church and a walk all in the bargain! The walk, too, will detain you for rather longer that its length might suggest. Not only are there expansive views at every turn, there is also a final climb of over 250 ft to negotiate.

An early guidebook described Snowshill's location quite vividly. It talked of the village being 'tucked tightly into a narrow combe in the side of a much larger combe'.

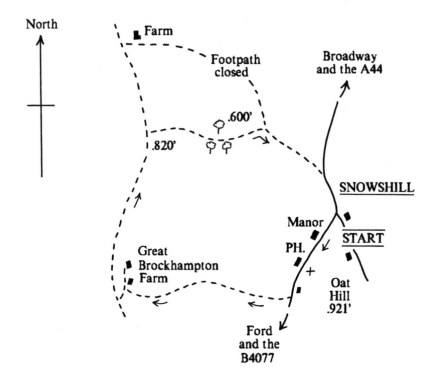

North

Farm

Footpath
closed

Broadway
and the A44

.600'

.820'

SNOWSHILL

Manor

PH.

START

Great
Brockhampton
Farm

Oat
Hill
.921'

Ford
and the
B4077

Not to scale.

The writer went on to comment that 'those who have experienced its lovely combination of valley and open wold quickly learn that Snowshill has charms denied to many places with more obvious claims'. This is one walk with few attractions other than the quite magnificent natural landscape. In a corner of the wolds that possesses such fine vistas, it is perhaps appropriate that there is little of peripheral interest to distract our attention.

The Walk

Continue along the road alongside the inn, past the rebuilt and somewhat disappointing church, until you come to Oat House and the edge of the village. On the right-hand side, just beyond Oat House, look out for a stone footpath marker and a gate. Follow the track beyond this gateway for 150 yards downhill to a second gate, and then continue ahead keeping a hedgerow on your right-hand side. The path is obvious and, beyond a stile, borders a plantation before emerging

18

at a second stile into an open meadow. This meadow, a sheep pasture, fills a secluded valley with a small stream at the foot of the hillside. The brooks and streamlets hereabouts drain northwards to flow into Shakespeare's Avon.

Cross the meadow, climbing its far side to reach a gate that lies 20 yards to the left of a farmhouse. Turn left beyond this gate, and follow a track for just a few yards to a metalled drive. Bear right, and follow this drive as it passes slightly above the complex of farm buildings. The views back towards Snowshill are quite breathtaking. From this perspective, its remote location at over 750 ft above sea level can be fully appreciated.

Continue along the driveway for about 200 yards to a stile in the wall on the right, alongside a footpath sign. This path is not shown on the OS map, being the result of a footpath diversion which has closed the path some 200 yards further on that originally led back to Snowshill. Cross the stile, and follow the right-hand field boundary beyond through some trees and on downhill towards the foot of the valley. A further stile brings you into some woodland, where the path bears to the right to descend to a wooden footbridge across a stream in the bottom of the valley.

Pass through the handgate beyond this bridge, and take the direction indicated by a yellow waymark, following the right-hand field boundary uphill away from the valley bottom. In 150 yards, look out for a stone-slab stile beneath an oak tree. Cross this stile, and head back towards Snowshill. Aim for the stile just 20 yards down from the top corner of the field ahead, and in the top corner of one last field you will join the road leading into the village. Turn right, and it is just a few minutes walk back to the Snowshill Arms and your car.

Stanton
The Mount

Stanton is an outstandingly beautiful village that nestles beneath the wooded Cotswold edge. The main village street climbs the lower slopes of the hills to reach the Mount Inn, a wholly appropriate name given its location on a small knoll. The most popular spot at the Mount is its terraced garden, with fine views that extend from the nearby village as far as the more distant Welsh Hills. Internally, the smaller original bar has been extended to accommodate the large number of visitors that have surprisingly discovered this isolated hostelry. As with so many Cotswold pubs, there is an abundance of stonework that includes a flagstone floor and a grand fireplace. Racing enthusiasts will find a fascinating collection of cigarette cards of Derby and Grand National winners, whilst the extensive display of local prints will perhaps enjoy a more widespread appeal.

The bar meals provided at the Mount are both good quality and of ample proportions. In addition to the normal sandwiches and ploughman's, more unusual offerings include cow pie and chicken and broccoli lasagne. Each day, a range of special dishes is also available. The Mount is a Donnington's inn, part of a small chain of Cotswold pubs owned and run by the Donnington Brewery based close to Stow-on-the-Wold. Donnington's have been brewing real ale for a good number of years, far longer in fact than the big brewers who only resumed the production of such brews following pressure from CAMRA. Not only is their beer of excellent quality, it is also very competitively priced. It is advisable not to comment on such a reasonably priced pint however – the landlady threatened to charge more for my second pint if I wasn't satisfied!

Telephone: Stanton (Glos) 316.

How to get there: Stanton lies just ½ mile off the B4632 (formerly A46) Broadway to Cheltenham road, 3 miles south of Broadway. As you enter the village, bear left along the main street, a cul-de-sac which terminates at the Mount Inn.

Parking: There is a car park for patrons to the rear of the Mount. Alternatively, there is roadside parking in the village below the inn.

Length of the walk: 5 miles. Map: OS Landranger 150 Worcester and the Malverns (GR 072342).

This walk encompasses two of the finest Cotswold villages – at Stanton and Stanway – where you will find examples of definitive Cotswold architecture. There is scarcely a building in Stanton that is not a delight to the eye, whether it be the well-proportioned Perpendicular church, the Court, the manor house or the picture-postcard cottages. All are lovingly fashioned from the golden local stone. Stanway is dominated by its fine manor house and its magnificent 17th century gatehouse. From these villages, a stiff climb of over 600 ft up through Lidcombe Wood brings us onto the high wolds. The view as the path descends back into Stanton at the end of the walk is quite exceptional, ranging as far afield as the Malvern Hills, the Shropshire Hills and the Welsh Mountains.

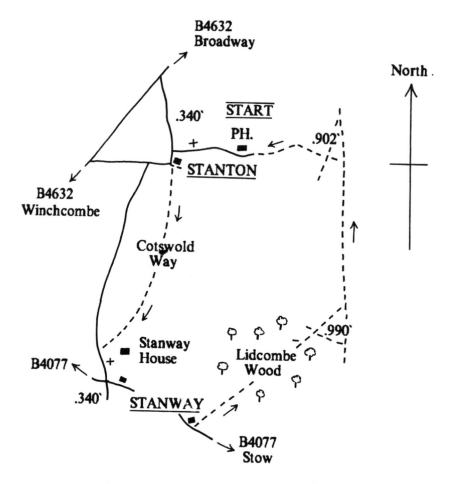

Not to scale.

The Walk

From the Mount Inn, walk back down Stanton's main street and turn left along the road signposted to Stanway. In just 200 yards, just beyond an ornate lantern that adorns the roadside on your left, turn left onto a track that leads up to Chestnut Farm. Opposite the farm, cross the stile on the right-hand side and follow the signposted Cotswold Way. Directions are unnecessary for the next mile, as the Cotswold Way contours the fields, meadows and parkland between

Stanton and Stanway – the right of way is well signposted as well as being well used. Simply enjoy the fine views to the west of this quiet corner of the northern Cotswolds. All too soon, the Cotswold Way joins a lane on the edge of Stanway. Opposite is the local cricket ground, with its most unusual thatched pavilion perched upon a fine collection of staddle stones. Turn left at the road, and continue through Stanway until you reach a crossroads and the B4077 Stow to Tewkesbury road. As well as passing Stanway House and its neighbouring gatehouse, look out for the bronze war memorial at the crossroads which depicts St George and the dragon.

Turn left, and follow the B4077 for ½ mile as it begins the ascent of the Cotswold escarpment. Where the road bears sharply to the right, keep straight on along an unmetalled lane that leads between some cottages towards Lidcombe Wood. Ahead the path forks – bear left to begin a climb of some 600 ft up through the woodland, Papermill Farm down in the valley on the left-hand side. Shortly, in a clearing, take the right-hand fork to follow the path on uphill through the trees for almost 1 mile, ignoring any side turnings, until it passes through a gateway at the top of the climb. At this point, the woods are still to your left whilst open fields appear on the right-hand side. In a short distance, just before some telegraph wires, the main path bears away to the right, a path comes in from the woods on the left, whilst between the two is a handgate and a bridlepath leading across a couple of arable fields. Cross these fields to a junction with another bridlepath, and turn left. You are now very firmly on the high wolds, with extensive views to the east. Particular landmarks that might catch your eye are the village of Snowshill and the more distant Broadway Tower. In ½ mile, just past an old quarry on the left-hand side, the bridlepath reaches an unmetalled lane. Turn left along this lane, ignore the Cotswold Way crossing in just a matter of yards, and quite literally follow the path for the next mile as it descends the hillside back into Stanton. The views ahead are magnificent, taking in the Malvern Hills, the Welsh Hills, the Shropshire Highlands and much else besides. The sunken path descends alongside field boundaries before passing through another old quarry, the remains resembling the ramparts of an old hillfort. Cross the stile below these workings, follow the enclosed path beyond and in just a few yards you will find yourself emerging alongside the Mount Inn.

Winchcombe
The White Hart

The White Hart is a Flowers inn, lying on Winchcombe's High Street. Its black-and-white timber framed construction is typical of many old buildings that enhance the Midland counties, a sure sign that at Winchcombe we are close to Gloucestershire's northern boundary. The only real concession to the Cotswold style of architecture is a roof fashioned out of the local stone. The small public bar and its adjoining lounge are both served from a central bar where, in addition to Flowers beers, Marston's and Boddingtons are on tap. The timber framed interior of the lounge bar is in keeping with its official title – the Elizabethan Bar.

Wooden tables and chairs, together with cushioned window seats, form the internal decoration of what is an unpretentious inn. The comfortable interior is completed by a stone fireplace, attractive lamps, a collection of rural prints and a number of iron farm implements from centuries past. These include several pairs of pincers together with a number of vicious looking animal traps.

The range of bar food is extensive, if a little routine. Starters include prawns, smoked mackerel and pate, whilst the main course dishes extend to cover salads and a number of grills. The varieties of salad include cheese, pork pie, chicken and boiled ham, whilst the grills cover chicken, rump and T-bone steaks. Also available are plaice, quiche, scampi, sea food platter and gammon dishes, together with meat and vegetable pie and various trout options. Sandwiches, ploughman's and a choice of sweets complete the White Hart's food fare. To the rear of the bar area is a pleasant dining room, where white tablecloths and a dresser laden with china create a homely atmosphere.

Unlike many Cotswold inns that have gone out of their way to attract the tourist trade at the expense of the locals and their needs, the White Hart is still very much a locals' pub. For walkers arriving in damp clothing, there are unlikely to be anxious glances from the bar about the reaction of the better-dressed patrons! A friendly hostelry where both locals and visitors alike are warmly welcomed.

Telephone: Cheltenham 602359.

How to get there: Winchcombe lies on what was the A46 trunk road (now the B4632) running north-eastwards from Cheltenham to Broadway. The White Hart is on the right-hand side, coming into the High Street from the Cheltenham direction, a short distance on from the church.

Parking: The White Hart fronts directly onto Winchcombe's High Street. Parking can therefore easily be found on the nearby streets.

Length of the walk: 5½ miles. Map: OS Landranger 150 Worcester and the Malverns (GR 025283).

The highest parts of the wolds lie in the north, between Cheltenham and Broadway. Cleeve Hill, for example, rises to 1,083 ft above sea level. The river Isbourne carves a path through this quite dramatic landscape, having its source on the slopes of Cleeve Hill, from where it flows northwards to join the Warwickshire Avon at Evesham. Sitting proudly at the head of the valley is the small town of Winchcombe. History is thick on the ground in what was once a Saxon walled city. After a reasonably strenuous climb onto the nearby Salter's Hill, the ramble drops down to another site of great antiquity – the ruins of the Cistercian abbey at Hailes. Throughout, the views are far-ranging, with landmarks such as the Vale of Evesham reminding us that this is border country. The Worcestershire border lies just 5 miles north of Winchcombe at Wormington.

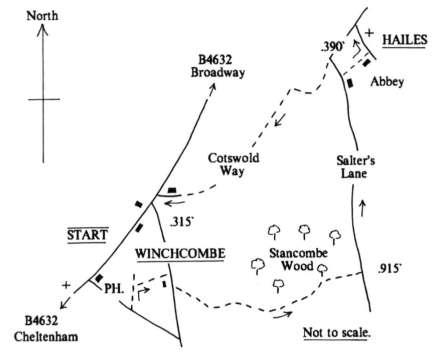

The Walk

Turn into Castle Street, the turning that runs alongside the White Hart. Cross the Isbourne at the foot of the hill and, within a matter of yards, turn left along a narrow alley between Tan Yard Bank and Sudeley Mill Cottage. At the end of this alley, pass through a kissing-gate and cross the sheep pasture diagonally to the right. The right-hand side of the field dips down to a lane which you join after passing through a small handgate.

Turn right, and in 100 yards a public footpath is signposted into a field on the left-hand side. The route lies uphill, across the fields that now lie ahead, passing to the right of Stancombe Wood. In the first field, aim for the stile diagonally to the right, just along from a gateway. In the next field, bear half-left to reach a gateway in the opposite hedgerow. In the third field, it is half-right to a gateway opposite. In fact, the right of way is so clearly waymarked that these complex sounding directions are probably unnecessary! From here to the hilltop, literally follow the left-hand field boundaries, always keeping Stancombe Wood to your left, and aiming for the steady succession of stiles with their clearly marked direction arrows. The climb brings rewarding views back across Winchcombe, with Cleeve Hill rising impressively in the background. Sudeley Castle is another prominent landmark. Right on the hilltop, the path bears to the left and passes through a gateway into an arable field. Follow the wall on the right onto a track and thence onto Salter's Lane. The climb up from Winchcombe to this ancient saltway has been a good 500 ft!

Turn left and follow the lane downhill towards Hailes, with fine views opening up northwards towards the Vale of Evesham. At the bottom of the hill, just past a group of cottages, turn right onto a gravelled track which leads past a few more cottages and into an open field. Hailes Abbey is located at the far side of this field. Cross to a stile, just to the left of the ruins, and join the cul-de-sac lane that leads to the abbey. Both the church and the ruins of the Cistercian abbey, now cared for by English Heritage, are worth an hour of your time.

To return to Winchcombe, follow the lane away from the abbey, past the church and onto a road junction. Turn left, cross a tributary stream of the Isbourne, and where the lane bears sharply to the left continue straight ahead along a waymarked bridlepath. In a few hundred yards, turn right onto another path, with a pair of fine old oak trees to your right. It is not long before the right of way bears to the left across an arable field, white discs on marker posts indicating the direction of the footpath. You are now actually following a section of the Cotswold Way, and the path is consequently well-used and well-signposted.

After a kissing-gate, bear half-right towards the distant telegraph wires. Beyond the next kissing-gate, the path rises and Winchcombe comes into view ahead. If you are walking the route on a Bank Holiday or a summer weekend, a very evocative sight might appear to your right as steam engines regularly ply the preserved section of the Gloucestershire and Warwickshire Railway – another GWR! Drop down to a footbridge, beyond which you join Puck Pit Lane. This leads in ½ mile to the B4632. Turn left, and follow the pavement alongside the main road back into Winchcombe. In ten minutes you will be in the centre of the town outside the White Hart.

Naunton
The Black Horse

Naunton is a long thin village spread out along the floor of the Windrush valley. The Black Horse Inn, dating from 1870, lies almost at the eastern end of the village's main street, almost ¾ mile from the parish church on the western edge of Naunton. Whether there is any significance in this physical separation of the alehouse from the house of worship I don't know. Certainly parishioners would be hard put to manage the morning service and a pint before Sunday lunch! An earlier hostelry – the Naunton Inn – existed in the village until 1910. This former coaching inn then became a farmhouse.

The Black Horse is a small compact inn, formed as an L-shaped building. The furnishings – country-kitchen chairs, oak pews and iron-framed elm tables – provide a traditional ambience that matches the inn's flagstone flooring, black beams and exposed stonework. A large wood-burning stove warms the interior of the Black Horse during winter months, whilst in the summer patrons can enjoy the sun's warmth from a small number of tables at the front of the inn. There is no garden as such, the tables fronting onto the village's main street, although 'main' must be interpreted in the context of the rural Cotswolds!

The regular meals on offer are the usual pub fare – home-made soup, pate, ploughman's lunches, ham, chicken and gammon – whilst daily specials might include rather more unusual choices of food such as marinated herring fillets, roast duckling, beef casserole and salmon salad. This range of special dishes also extends to the sweets, which have included lemon brulee and chocolate trufito. The Black Horse is a Donnington's house, Donnington's being a local brewery situated in an idyllic location alongside a millpond in a village near Stow. The well-painted black and white inn signs, the brewery's trademark, are a familiar landmark in several Cotswold villages. Both the Donnington BB and SBA are available at the Black Horse. A better pint in equally convivial surroundings would be difficult to find.

Telephone: Cotswold (0451) 850378.

How to get there: Naunton lies 6 miles west of Stow-on-the-Wold, just north of the B4068 road that links Stow with the A436. Follow an unclassified road into Naunton from the east, and the Black Horse is on the right-hand side just as you enter the village.

Parking: There is a small car park alongside the Black Horse. The limited parking, however, means that walkers are better advised to park on the village's main street.

Length of the walk: 6½ miles. Map: OS Landranger 163 Cheltenham and Cirencester (GR 121234).

This relatively long walk encapsulates the very best of what the Cotswolds have to offer. Naunton and Upper Slaughter are two of the finest stone villages in the wolds, both nestling in sheltered river valleys. At Naunton it is the Windrush, whilst at Upper Slaughter the Eye. Above these villages lie the high wolds, open hilltops that offer fine views across rolling countryside and down into wooded valleys. An excellent circuit that will linger long in the memory.

The Walk
From the Black Horse, walk westwards along Naunton's main street for 200 yards. Just before a road turns off on the right, turn left along a path that crosses the river Windrush before reaching open fields. Follow the right-hand field boundaries uphill through the next couple of fields to reach the B4068. Turn right along this quiet road for 150 yards, with fine views of Naunton nestling in the valley to the north, before turning left onto a signposted public bridlepath. Follow this path across the hilltop and down into the next valley, which carries a small unnamed tributary of the Windrush. Cross the stream using the

conveniently placed stone slab, and turn immediately left through a handgate into the adjoining riverside field. Follow the well-used path along the floor of the valley, through three fields, until you reach a quiet country lane.

Turn left at the lane, and a delightful sight awaits you. A ford carries the lane through the sparkling waters of the Windrush, in front of Hartford Farm. Follow the lane to the left in front of the farmhouse and, almost straightaway, pass through a gateway on the right-hand side. Follow a waymarked field-path uphill to the top right-hand corner of the field, and continue along the top edge of the next field until you emerge onto a country lane. Follow this lane eastwards for over 1 mile until it joins the Naunton to Bourton road. The lane is extemely quiet – the local Post Office van and farm vehicles probably its main users – as it crosses the hills to the north of the Windrush. The views down into the heavily wooded valley are quite superb, and rail buffs might well spot the old railway leading to Bourton-on-the-Water clinging to the opposite hillside.

At the road junction, cross straight over and follow a gravelled drive for 100 yards to a gate. Follow the sheep pasture beyond to its far end, where a bewildering choice of four gateways awaits you. Pass through the one that is second from the left, and follow the field boundary beyond to the left down into Upper Slaughter. This path brings excellent views into the Eye valley, in which Upper Slaughter nestles most picturesquely. At the foot of the hill, the path meets a road. Cross straight over and follow the lane into Upper Slaughter, where the usual combination of church, manor and picture-postcard cottages will undoubtedly catch the eye. Just past the Lord of the Manor Hotel and Restaurant on the right, turn left along a lane signposted as 'Unsuitable for Motor Vehicles' and 'Ford'. As the lane drops down to the ford, turn left along a track that runs between the church and the Eye. The ford is a quintessentially English scene, and is a memory that all visitors will take with them.

Follow the gravelled track through a wooded area alongside the river and on to a gateway and open countryside beyond. Follow the right-hand field boundaries of the next two fields until you reach an isolated cottage, beyond which the path enters an area of woodland high above the Eye. The next ½ mile is an all too short stretch of the most exquisite woodland walking, as the path runs alongside the Eye before joining the B4068 Stow road. Turn left, and follow the verge for ¼ mile before bearing right along a signposted bridlepath that runs along the side of a rank of cottages. Beyond the gate, some 100 yards on, follow the left-hand field boundary to the top corner of the field and another gate. As this field-path climbs the slope ahead, fine views

30

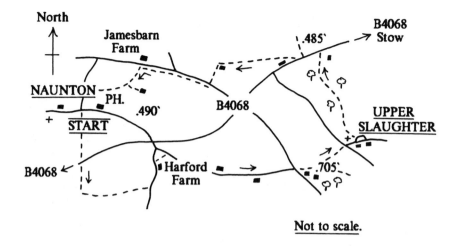

Not to scale.

open up to the north of the Eye valley. Head directly across the next three fields, a well-worn path and gateways indicating the right of way, until you reach a barn. The path continues to the left behind the barn, to join a lane opposite Brockhill Quarry. Cross the road, pass through the handgate opposite, and turn sharp right. Follow the field boundaries through the next three fields, all the while running a course that is parallel to the road network the other side of the hedge. The path rejoins the road alongside Jamesbarn Farm.

Turn immediately to the left along a signposted bridlepath that heads across the hilltop before dropping into a small dip. Where the track bears to the left to Hill Barn, continue straight ahead to the corner of the field. The path passes through a small wooded area to emerge in an open field. Head across the centre of the next couple of fields, along a well-worn path that gradually bears to the right. In a third field, the path bears to the left to descend into a strip of woodland that lies above Naunton. Pass through the trees, and you will emerge into one final hillside field above the village, spread out in the valley below. The path slopes down to the far side of the field, passing a magnificent collection of chestnut trees, where you join a lane leading into Naunton. At the junction ahead, turn left to retrace your steps to the Black Horse.

NB. Lengthy stretches of this walk, especially the return leg from Upper Slaughter to Naunton, follow the well-signposted Warden's Way footpath. It is not easy to lose your way!

Brockhampton
The Craven Arms

The Craven Arms is a delightful pub, enjoying a quiet location at the end of a cul-de-sac lane in one of the Cotswolds' less well known corners. The inn dates back as far as the 17th century, and is beautifully fashioned out of the mellow local stone. Unlike some of the Cotswold inns, there have been no attempts to plaster or whitewash the Craven Arms – it is pure unadulterated limestone! Internally, there is a series of spacious inter-connected rooms, with an abundance of low beams and exposed stonework. When combined with the flagstone flooring, the pine furniture and the open fireplaces, the overall effect is to create a warm and welcoming atmosphere in an inn that possesses a distinctly rural feel. This is enhanced by old agricultural implements hanging from the walls and ceilings of the inn. To the rear of the Craven Arms is a sunny garden, surrounded by attractive flower borders, where a number of picnic tables enable patrons to enjoy the local Cotswold air.

Bar food at the inn is freshly prepared, and the day's offerings are displayed on a blackboard in the bar area. An interesting array of dishes is normally available, as was evident on a recent visit. French onion soup, avocado filled with prawns, king prawns in garlic butter, garlic smoked mackerel . . . a selection of dishes to whet your appetite! Less adventurous palates are well catered for, too, with ploughman's lunches, grills and the traditional steak and kidney pie. The sweets on offer are enough to give slimmers a nightmare – treacle tart, sticky toffee pudding, banana and peach crumble and chocolate fudge cake are but examples of the many delicious concoctions available. To make matters worse, all of the sweets were being served with lashings of double cream. Sunday lunchtime sees the menu more restricted, with the focus on traditional roast meals.

Finally, of course, the beers. The Craven Arms is a freehouse and the excellence of the cuisine is matched by the fine ales available. Two independent brewers – Butcombe and Hook Norton – have beers on tap, whilst enthusiasts of the Devizes-based Wadworth brewery will not be disappointed.

Telephone: Cheltenham 820410.

How to get there: Brockhampton lies on the unclassified road that runs across the wolds from the A40 at Andoversford to Winchcombe. The signposted Craven Arms lies at the end of a cul-de-sac lane in the middle of the village.

Parking: There is a car park for patrons at the rear of the Craven Arms. The narrow village lanes offer few parking places.

Length of the walk: 3 miles. Map: OS Landranger 163 Cheltenham and Cirencester (GR 035223).

This walk is deliberately low on miles to enable you not only to enjoy the first class Craven Arms inn, but also because of the magnificent man-made and natural landscape that will delay your steps. The two villages on the route – Sevenhampton and Brockhampton – are not names that most visitors to the Cotswolds will be familiar with. Lying along unclassified lanes, far from the nearest main road, both villages take some finding and are all the better for that. Their stone cottages, the inn and St Andrew's church at Sevenhampton, lie scattered along the upper reaches of the Coln valley, hereabouts little more than a small stream. As well as an exploration of these settlements, the walk takes us high on to the wolds above the valley. Here, at over 800 ft above sea level, we follow an ancient bridlepath that brings with it extensive views across a particularly evocative part of the Cotswolds.

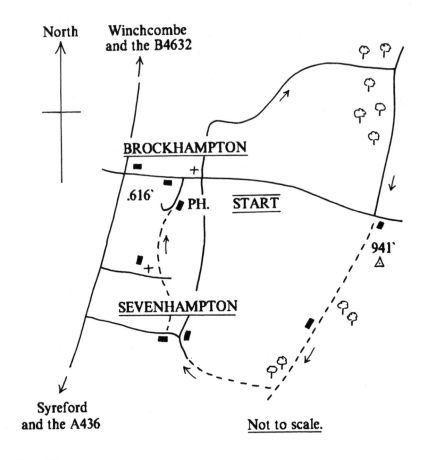

North

Winchcombe
and the B4632

BROCKHAMPTON

.616'

PH.   START

941'

SEVENHAMPTON

Syreford
and the A436

Not to scale.

The Walk

Retrace your steps along the lane away from the Craven Arms, turn
right at the junction a short distance from the inn, and left at the
nearby crossroads alongside an old chapel. Follow the lane ahead for
1 mile, as it leaves Brockhampton and continues on through wooded
countryside to a T-junction. The signpost indicates that the lane to the
left leads to Guiting Power and Winchcombe, whilst we turn right to
follow the Andoversford and Stow turning.

   In ¾ mile, at another T-junction, head straight across onto a
bridlepath. This path heads across the open wolds, bringing fine views
to the west across the upper Coln valley. In ½ mile, you will pass a
traditional stone barn on the right-hand side, just before the path
begins its descent of the hillside. In a short distance, just beyond a

34

small patch of woodland on the right-hand side, you will see a gateway with a faded sign asking horse-riders to close the gate after use. Head through this gateway, and continue downhill towards the village of Sevenhampton in the valley. Follow the field boundaries through three fields to an enclosed track that bears right into the village.

A little way past the first few attractive cottages, you reach a minor road junction. The road ahead – unsuitable for motor vehicles – provides one route back to Brockhampton. A more interesting alternative is to turn left down to the ford through the waters of the Coln. Just before the ford, follow the footpath on the right signposted to Brockhampton, via St Andrew's church. The path literally borders the Coln for 100 yards, before crossing its waters and climbing uphill to the left. At the top of the rise, cross the open field to the clearly visible church. Alongside this Norman building lies the manor house, with one ruinous wing looking every bit the setting for a Dracula movie! Pass to the right of the church, and down to what is effectively an extension to the churchyard. In the corner of this burial area, continue through a kissing-gate and follow the left-hand boundary wall across the next field. The village of Brockhampton comes into view just ¼ mile ahead. Cross one final open field, using the houses and a prominent red-brick chimney stack in Brockhampton as a target. At the far side of the field, at the bottom of a dip, pass through a handgate and cross the infant river Coln. A path continues through the wilderness beyond to emerge alongside the Craven Arms and that chimney stack. The stack, incidentally represents the most visible remains of an old steam mill.

Coberley
The Seven Springs

The Seven Springs is named after a collection of springs that bubble out of the ground on the opposite side of the busy A436 to the inn. It has been claimed by some locals that this is the source of the Thames – in fact it is the source of the Churn, a mere tributary of the great river. The inn represents a conversion of what was previously a vast stone barn. It has been extensively reworked and modernised, although the interior does contain a convincing array of red-brick, exposed stone and wooden roof timbers.

The Seven Springs is a roadside hostelry, serving passing trade and tourists rather than a local community. In addition to the bar area, there is a large dining room on a lower level, a fine gallery and a conservatory attached to the rear of the building. It has all been designed on an open-plan principle. The conservatory overlooks a lawn that slopes down to a duck pond, where patrons drinking outdoors will have feathered companions! Around the walls inside are displayed a number of antiquarian photographs of local scenes, whilst at the far side of the dining room is a fine wood burning fire and a splendid pile of logs. The grand piano at the far side of the lounge bar is not just a show-piece. Patrons are regularly entertained by the house pianist, who occasionally doubles-up on the organ.

An extensive menu is offered at the Seven Springs Inn, that includes starters, fish dishes, grills, vegetarian dishes, cold fare, ploughman's and sweets. For an unusual starter, you might care to try crab claws and spicy prawns, or perhaps chicken satay. Vegetarians might be tempted by nasi goreng, korma curry or lentil crumble, whilst a Brie ploughman's represents a change from the usual Stilton or Cheddar. Traditionalists could devour a 16oz prime rump steak, with a choice of sauces that includes the inn's very own Seven Springs Sauce! The sweets, all served with freshly whipped cream, include deep dish apple pie, lemon sorbet, strawberry gateau and chocolate chocolate chocolate cake (no – this is not a misprint!). Daily specials are also chalked up in the bar. Being a Courage inn, both Courage Bitter and Directors are on tap. Alternative brews include Beamish Irish Stout, John Smith's Yorkshire Bitter, Wadworth 6X and a Simonds Bitter. As a final touch, teetotallers can enjoy a pot of tea, a beverage that non-coffee drinkers find annoyingly elusive in pubs and inns.

Telephone: Coberley 219.

How to get there: The Seven Springs Inn lies 4 miles south of Cheltenham, on the A435 Cirencester road, at its junction with the A436.

Parking: There is a large car park to the side of the inn. On the opposite side of the A436, alongside the Seven Springs, is a lay-by.

Length of the walk: 3 miles. Map: OS Landranger 163 Cheltenham and Cirencester (GR 967169).

A debate in Parliament was needed before the residents living around Seven Springs would give up its claim to being the source of Old Father Thames. Although Thames Head near Cirencester is officially the source of the river, there are certainly arguments for supporting the rival claims of Seven Springs. Seven Springs is the highest and furthest source from the mouth of the Thames, although in practice this is the source of the Churn, a mere tributary of Isis. This short walk explores the upper Churn valley between Seven Springs and Coberley, before it climbs to Upper Coberley, where hilltops bring fine views across this corner of the hills. In Coberley village is a charming group of buildings formed by the manor house and its attendant farm. Just behind them, through an archway, lies St Giles' church. With the farmyard buildings on one side of the church gate and the trim lawn of the house on the other side, this makes a quite delightful setting.

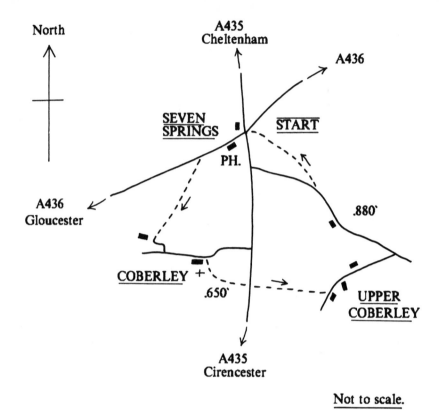

North

A435
Cheltenham

A436

SEVEN
SPRINGS

START

PH.

A436
Gloucester

.880'

COBERLEY +

.650'

UPPER
COBERLEY

A435
Cirencester

Not to scale.

The Walk

From the Seven Springs Inn, follow the busy A436 westwards for just 150 yards until you reach a kissing-gate on the left-hand side. Follow the enclosed path beyond this gate, as it crosses sheep pastures above the village of Coberley. In ¼ mile, cross a stile into an arable field and follow the bridlepath directly ahead all of the way down into Coberley village. The path eventually merges into a lane, which bears to the left in front of Yew Tree Cottage to reach a junction. Turn left and head out of the village. In ¼ mile you will pass Coberley Court and St Giles' church, by far the most interesting corner of Coberley. To reach the church, you actually have to pass through a small signposted door in the wall of what appears to be the local farmhouse – you will feel every bit the intruder! As well as a 'heart burial' – a local nobleman Sir Giles Berkeley was killed abroad but his heart was returned to his home village in 1295 for burial – the church has connections with a certain Richard Whittington, who later became Lord Mayor of London.

Immediately past the farm, turn right into a field to follow a waymarked path. This crosses a couple of fields that border the Court and the church, before passing through a small strip of woodland to reach a large open field. Head half-left across this field to reach a stile on the far side, about 20 yards to the left of a large prominent ash tree. Beyond the stile, cross the busy A435 with extreme care, and continue along the bridlepath waymarked on the opposite side of the road. It heads directly across an open field, passes through a gap in the hedge about 100 yards below a prominent detached house, and continues in the same direction across the next field. At the far side of this field, the path continues through an area of scrubland to reach a gate and the lane leading into Upper Coberley.

Upper Coberley is smaller than its neighbour, and is nothing more than a hamlet overlooking the Churn valley. Several fine open barns are testimony to the agricultural roots of this settlement. Pass through the hamlet to a road junction 200 yards on from the last farm – Upper Coberley Farm. Turn left, and follow a quiet lane across the hilltop for ½ mile until, a little way beyond New Farm Bungalow, you leave the lane and fork right onto a path signposted 'Bridlepath to Cotswold Way'. Follow this path for ½ mile back down into Seven Springs, not without first appreciating the extensive views to the west across the upper Churn valley towards South Hill.

Cold Aston
The Plough

Cold Aston presents an archetypal Cotswold scene – a delightful village green dominated by a vast sycamore tree, stone cottages and houses of various dimensions and sizes, the Georgian Sycamore House and the diminutive Plough Inn. This is quite literally a hostelry where the old adage about there not being enough room to swing a cat is wholly appropriate. There is essentially one bar in the 17th century Plough, with all manner of alcoves and corners that create a homely atmosphere. The ceiling is low – extremely low – and is supported by even lower black beams, whilst the flooring is traditional flagstone. A visit in midwinter would see the Plough warmed through by a most welcoming open fire, just the job after a stroll on the surrounding high wolds. By way of contrast, summer visitors can enjoy the fresh air on a small area of picnic tables just outside the inn.

The Plough is a freehouse, and various ales might be found on tap. Wadworth IPA, Fosters, John Smith's Yorkshire Bitter and Blackthorn Dry cider are all usually to hand. The bar food is excellent, and changes with great frequency. The day's offerings are chalked alongside the bar. As well as a varied selection of ploughman's lunches, including a fine Stilton, there is a good variety of stuffed jacket potatoes. The fillings could include tuna or a most tempting ham and sweetcorn. Other hot dishes on my most recent visit included seafood lasagne, cauliflower cheese, cottage pie and chilli con carne. The dishes are both ample and well-presented, a nice touch on the ploughman's, for example, being slices of apple and orange.

The Plough is one of those places to just laze and relax after a Cotswold ramble – a sign alongside the bar announces to all and sundry that this is a 'slow food' hostelry. If you are in a hurry, you are recommended to rush off to some less welcoming fast food outlet! Given the relaxed and cosy surroundings, this would be one inn where a delay would not be unwelcome.

Telephone: Cotswold (0451) 821459.

How to get there: Cold Aston lies just 1 mile west of the A429 between Northleach and Bourton-on-the-Water. The Plough lies alongside the green in the centre of the village.

Parking: There is a car park to the rear of the Plough, as well as ample parking on the lanes alongside the inn.

Length of the walk: 5 miles. Map: OS Landranger 163 Cheltenham and Cirencester (GR 129197).

This undulating ramble crosses the high wolds above Northleach, where extensive views are ample compensation for the relatively gentle climbs that have to be undertaken. The three villages on the route – Cold Aston, Notgrove and Turkdean – are typical of the Cotswold uplands and, lying off the main tourist axis, enjoy an ordinariness that has been lost in much of the area. The very absence of museums, gift shops and tea rooms is a blessing in disguise! The sole attractions are those very things that thoughtful visitors to the wolds expect – stone villages, ancient churches, deep valleys, steep hillsides and hard working farms.

The Walk
From the Plough, turn left and follow the road signposted to Notgrove. In approximately ½ mile, just beyond the edge of Cold Aston village, you will reach a fine avenue of beech trees on the left-hand side. Turn left at this point through a handgate, and follow a bridlepath through the trees for just over ½ mile until the path joins a farm track. Turn right and, in just 20 yards, cross a gate into a field on the left-hand side. The village of Notgrove lies down below in the valley.

41

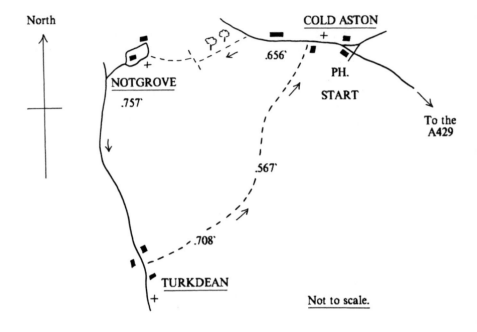

Head downhill across the middle of the field, and continue up the slope beyond to a gateway that lies 100 yards to the right of the church. The stone spire of this Norman building acts as a fine landmark. Beyond the gateway, a detour to the left will bring you into the churchyard, whilst our route lies to the right along the upper of two roads that meet at this point. Continue along this road, passing Manor Farm and the village cricket pitch, until you reach a road junction. Turn left and follow a quiet country lane across the high wolds for 1½ miles to Turkdean. This is road walking, but you will be unfortunate if you encounter more than a dozen vehicles. Fine views extend in all directions, with no particular landmarks. It is simply an excellent rural landscape.

The road eventually descends into Turkdean, where a left turn is taken just as you enter the village. This turning lies opposite some farm buildings and is signposted as being 'unsuitable for motor vehicles'. Another detour will be needed should you wish to explore Turkdean's Norman church and the centre of the village.

The path – a bridlepath – is followed for a couple of miles back to Cold Aston, dropping down into one prominent valley en route. 'Progress' has clearly affected this part of the wolds as sheep farming

42

has been replaced by cereal production. The old pastures have fallen victim to the plough, whilst many lengths of stone wall have been dismantled to provide building materials, to be replaced by functional wire fencing. The bridlepath joins the Cold Aston to Notgrove road just a few hundred yards west of the Plough. Turn right at the road to retrace your steps to the inn.

Northleach
The Red Lion

Northleach was one of the great Cotswold wool towns during the heyday of the local cloth trade, and no doubt much of the town's commerce took place in the Market Place. The Red Lion, along with the Union and the Sherborne Arms, would have been popular watering holes with the local traders following a hard morning's buying and selling. The black-and-white exterior of the Red Lion would not go amiss further north in Herefordshire, a county renowned for its timber framed constructions of similar ilk. It is only the Cotswold stone roof that gives away the Lion's location.

Internally, this is a good old-fashioned local. There is one main bar – small and intimate – with a raised open fireplace and exposed black beams. Some original stonework has been opened up in the bar, where the main decorations are a number of pieces of china and a collection of photographs. Behind the bar area is a dining room, offering a quieter atmosphere than in the popular 'front room'.

This is a Courage house, with both their Best Bitter and Directors Bitter on tap, although the choice of ales also extends to other brews such as John Smith's Yorkshire Bitter and Beamish Irish Stout. The bar food is simple and traditional and comes well presented in good portions. Starters, ploughman's, salads, sandwiches, fish dishes, jacket potatoes, children's dishes and desserts are all available, as well as daily specials that are chalked up on boards.

Telephone: Cotswold 60251.

How to get there: Northleach lies just off the A429 Fosse Way, between Cirencester and Stow-on-the-Wold. The town is clearly signposted from the main road, with the Red Lion lying on the northern side of the Market Place.

Parking: Park on the road outside the inn, or on the central parking area of the Market Place which is directly opposite.

Length of the walk: 3 miles. Map: OS Landranger 163 Cheltenham and Cirencester (GR 114146).

The river Leach is one of the Cotswolds' noted rivers, flowing south-eastwards through the area to join the Thames at Lechlade. This walk explores the infant river between Northleach and Hampnett, as well as covering the higher wolds to the south of the river valley. Further interest is added by the fine churches at both Northleach and Hampnett, the latter possessing a controversial set of stencil decorations painted onto the walls by a 19th century clergyman.

45

The Walk

From the Red Lion and the Market Place in Northleach, return to the A429 by walking in a north-westerly direction along the High Street. Cross the A429 and continue along the unclassified road opposite, past a former 'house of correction' that now houses a museum of rural life. After the walk, it is well worth returning to the museum to enjoy the fascinating displays. These include the restored county prison, where five year olds could be gaoled for being found to be 'rogues and vagabonds'. Just past the museum, cross the stile on the right-hand side and follow the perimeter of the field beyond to its far left-hand corner where a footbridge crosses what appears to be nothing more than a tiny stream. This is in fact the river Leach within 1 mile of its source. Continue around the next field to a stile in the top left-hand corner, just alongside the edge of a small area of woodland known as Priston Copse. Beyond this stile, climb uphill as you make for the far right-hand corner of the field, where a short length of farm track on the right brings you onto the Hampnett road. Turn left, and continue into the village less than ¼ mile ahead.

The walk follows a bridlepath on the left just as you enter Hampnett, although you will probably want to continue the few yards to visit the church. A Victorian vicar – the Reverend Wiggin – attempted to produce a replica of a medieval church here around 1871 by stencilling the walls with some quite eye-catching designs. Despite attempts a few years ago to expunge Wiggin's creation, the stencil designs still remain and attract polarised reactions from visitors!

Returning to the previously mentioned bridlepath, continue downhill past a cattle byre and a pond to a junction, where you turn left to follow a bridlepath that climbs the far side of the Leach valley before it joins a quiet country road. Continue straight across, following the right-hand field boundary in the opposite field until you reach another quiet lane alongside a waterboard installation. These high wolds above Northleach have been rather spoiled by 20th century man's handiwork. A set of ugly pylons stand as a vast scar on the landscape, whilst the heavy traffic on the nearby A429 is admittedly rather intrusive.

Turn left at the road, and in another 150 yards left again at a minor crossroads along the road signposted to Northleach and Stow-on-the-Wold. Continue along this lane between its fine drystone walls to the A429, and cross straight over along the lane signposted to Mill End. There is one final short section of road walking past an electricity sub-station on the left, before you turn left immediately past a small copse to descend into a delightful river valley, a tributary of the Leach. Follow the river downstream for 200 yards as it splashes through most

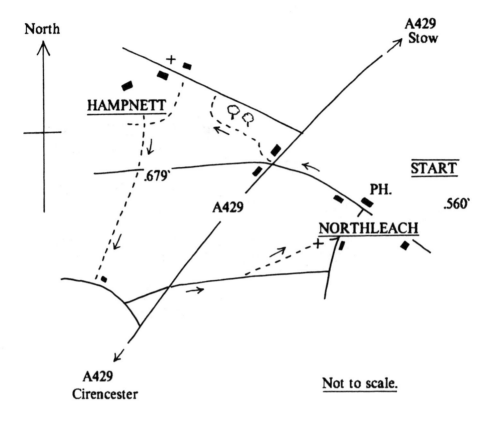

North

A429
Stow

HAMPNETT

.679'

A429

START

PH.

.560'

NORTHLEACH

A429
Cirencester

Not to scale.

attractive sheep pasture, before crossing to the far bank on a small
footbridge. Once across the bridge, bear right towards the churchyard
wall of the now very prominent Northleach church. Aim for the top
end of the facing wall, turn right and continue following the wall until
you reach a small kissing-gate that leads into the churchyard. This is
one of the finest churches in the Cotswolds, financed, naturally, out
of the area's woollen wealth. The church was entirely rebuilt in the
15th century, and is Perpendicular design at its very best. Brass
rubbers will find an excellent set of wool merchants' brasses within
the church, whilst students of ecclesiastical architecture will admire
the fine stone pulpit.

The northern exit from the churchyard brings you onto a road
which is followed for just a few minutes into the centre of Northleach
and the town's Market Place.

Chedworth
The Seven Tuns

The Seven Tuns is a stone-built freehouse, set in the most attractive part of Chedworth village just below St Andrew's church. The hillsides roundabout are dotted with cottages linked by a network of lanes, a settlement that clearly grew up before the age of the motor car. This up-and-down nature of the village has been described perfectly by one commentator who said 'it is not a place for the rabid road-hog who would be distressed to find himself looking up to a doorstep and down on a chimney'. Down one of these sloping lanes lies the Seven Tuns Inn.

Tuns are, of course, brewers' fermenting vats, which gives a clue as to the origins of the inn. The spring that bubbles out of the wall across the road from the Seven Tuns would certainly have provided a water supply for any would-be brewer. This can, however, be but speculation.

The lounge bar is quite a tidy affair, with a cosy and welcoming atmosphere. Like many a Cotswold pub, there is a fine stone fireplace that houses a roaring log fire in winter months, whilst a number of prints and a collection of tankards add to the atmosphere. The public bar is more down-to-earth, and is perhaps a better option for walkers fresh from their exertions in the surrounding countryside. Above the bar, a collection of bank notes from all around the world is displayed, whilst on one of the walls is a fascinating collection of old local photographs. These include pictures of the long-gone Chedworth railway station, the Chedworth Home Guard in the 1940s and a local winter scene that looks every bit like the winter of 1963. A number of photos show local characters from years past, in most cases supping at their local! Outside the inn, a side terrace provides the setting for picnic table sets, whilst across the road is a smaller terrace.

A full range of bar food is available at the Seven Tuns. Light meals could include the home-made pate, sandwiches or ploughman's, whilst a more substantial meal could be chosen from such selections as steak and kidney pie, sea food gratin, smoked mackerel or moussaka. Children are well catered for with their own range of basket meals, and there is also a vegetarian dish available. Daily specials are also chalked up on a board. These might include such dishes as quiche, seafood pancakes, smoked mackerel pate and vegetable chilli. The sweets form, perhaps, the most popular part of the menu, with such irresistible choices as jam roly-poly pudding, blackberry and apple pie and profiteroles. The house beers include Courage Best and Directors, the original gravity of 1046 making it one of the stronger beers brewed by a national combine. Bed and breakfast is available from May to September. Telephone 0285 720242.

Incidentally, the Seven Tuns is located in Queen Street which does indeed have very regal origins. In 1491, when Elizabeth of York, wife of Henry VII, came to Chedworth to visit her royal aunts and the newly restored church, she stayed at the manor which already belonged to her husband. The medieval street which is now known as Queen Street records this visit, and its many 17th century buildings include the Seven Tuns Inn – 1610 is the date that appears on the inn.

How to get there: Seven miles north of Cirencester on the A429 Stow-on-the-Wold road, Chedworth village is signposted as a left-turn. Do not follow the signs for Chedworth Roman Villa, which lies some way from the village. As you enter Chedworth, the second signposted right-turn takes you into Queen Street, and the Seven Tuns lies just under ½ mile down the lane on the left-hand side.

Parking: The Seven Tuns does have a car park for patrons. There is also room for careful roadside parking up the hill beside St Andrew's church.

Length of the walk: 4 miles. Map: OS Landranger 163 Cheltenham and Cirencester (GR 053120).

The beauty of the Cotswold Hills has as much to do with human influence as with the natural landscape. The pastureland, the woodland and the river valleys are complemented by drystone walls, scattered farmsteads and picture-book villages, all lovingly crafted from the golden Cotswold stone. This ramble around the Chedworth area represents a perfect microcosm of the Cotswold Hills. The village itself lies in a tributary valley of the Coln. Above its cottages and roof-tops are the high wolds, undulating, open and exposed, whilst to the north lie the upper reaches of the Coln valley, where ancient woodland has maintained its hold to this day. On the edge of Chedworth Woods lies one of the country's finest Roman relics – Chedworth Roman Villa – now a National Trust property with public access.

The Walk

From the Seven Tuns, follow the road through the village away from the church. This road climbs steeply out of the village, and around a couple of bends before it emerges onto the level hilltop. There are excellent views back across Chedworth, nestling in its valley. Ignore the signposted footpaths that lead to Chedworth Villa, continuing instead along the minor road to a collection of farm buildings on the left-hand side. Five hundred yards beyond this point, a signpost indicates that footpaths leave the road on both sides. Turn off to the left, and pass through a gateway to head straight across the arable field ahead, towards Chedworth Woods. A prominent sycamore tree on the far side of the field is a good landmark.

Continue down the side of the woodland beyond this tree, to a gateway on the right that leads into the woods themselves. The next ½ mile is through a delightful area of mature mixed woodland, the floor a carpet of bluebells in April and May, and pheasants your constant companions. The wide woodland path emerges onto the Fossebridge to Yanworth road. Turn left, and where this road bears right to cross the Coln, continue straight ahead along a track signposted 'Private Road – Footpath Only'. This path continues for 1 mile with the Coln on its right and Chedworth Woods to the left, eventually emerging at a minor road junction, where you turn left to reach Chedworth Roman Villa.

Pass to the left of the entrance to Chedworth Villa and onto the footpath that leads into Chedworth Woods. You soon pass under an old railway bridge that carried the line from Cheltenham to Cirencester. The steps on the left lead up to the old track bed, now a nature reserve. Beyond the railway bridge, the path climbs gently to a cross-track. Turn left and follow the main path for almost ½ mile until it reaches a stile at the edge of the woodland. Ignore any minor paths or side turns. Cross a stile and follow the field-path directly ahead, passing over (or around) a couple of old stiles as far as a pair of handgates beneath a sycamore tree. As you cross the open fields from Chedworth Woods, there are fine views back northwards across the woodland and the Coln valley to the high wolds beyond.

Pass through the right-hand gate, cross the small field ahead to a stone stile and drop down a stepped path through a small patch of tree cover. Bear left along the meadow ahead. At the far end of this field, cross a stile alongside the cottage that comes into view on your right-hand side. Incidentally, hidden in the dense hedgerow on your left as you cross this meadow is the track bed encountered earlier. Since the bridge near to Chedworth Villa, it has passed through a short tunnel to avoid the climb that the walker has made! With the help of a decent map, industrial archaeologists may care to seek out its two entrances. The stile alongside the cottage brings you to the edge of Chedworth village. Continue along the road to the village church, and a left-turn will bring you back to the Seven Tuns.

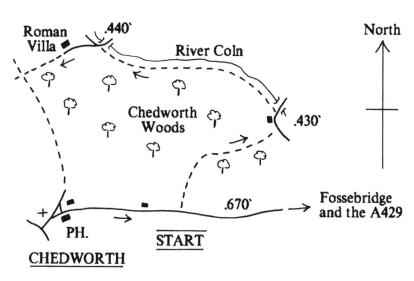

Not to scale.

North Cerney
The Bathurst Arms

The Bathurst Arms is a traditional Cotswold stone inn, although the golden stone of the walls has been lost beneath a coat of pink-wash and a covering of ivy. The inn has a delightful location – with the exception of the nearby main road – with its beer garden running down to the sparkling waters of the Churn. Internally, both Dickies Bar and the lounge share the same essential features – wooden tables and chairs, high backed wooden settles, wooden window seats, flagstone and board flooring and beams.

The Bathurst Arms has quite a reputation for its food, as is evident from a number of certificates and newspaper cuttings displayed in the lounge bar. The day's offerings are chalked up on several boards in the lounge, and include a number of quite unusual dishes when compared with usual pub fare.

The choice of beers is equally impressive. Old favourites like Bass and Wadworth are available, together with Archers from nearby Swindon and an interesting Bathurst Bitter. Archers brewery was set up in 1979 in an industrial unit in the former GWR rail works. The beers are produced using a 100% malt mash.

Telephone: North Cerney 281.

How to get there: North Cerney lies on the A435 Gloucester road, 4 miles north of Cirencester. The Bathurst Arms fronts onto the main road as you pass through the village.

Parking: There is a car park for patrons in front of the Bathurst Arms. Alternatively, there is ample room for roadside parking in the lane that runs alongside the inn.

Length of the walk: 6 miles. Map: OS Landranger 163 Cheltenham and Cirencester (GR 020079).

This relatively strenuous ramble explores a section of the Churn valley to the north of Cirencester. In both North Cerney and Bagendon, the two villages on the route, we find exquisite churches, both with saddleback towers. In the area to the east of Bagendon, lie the remains of the Iron Age capital of the Dobunni. Marked as Bagendon Dykes on the OS sheets, you will need to make a detour should you wish to seek out the few remains of this tribe that immediately pre-dated the Romans in Britain. From these hillsides above the Churn, the walk descends to the valley bottom where we follow the river back to North Cerney. For much of the way, its waters are hidden amongst bushes and undergrowth, but we are given a few all-too-brief glimpses of this delightful Cotswold river.

The Walk

Cross the road in front of the Bathurst Arms and follow the lane opposite signposted to Bagendon. On the left as you leave North Cerney is the village church, essentially Norman in origin and with a quite beautiful saddleback tower. Continue up the hill out of North Cerney, passing the entrance to Cerney House on your right. At a crossroads, head straight across and in ½ mile you will find yourself at a junction on the edge of the village. On the right is the local war memorial which records the fact that eleven men from the village laid down their lives during the First World War – a staggering number given the small size of the settlement. Turn left, and in a short distance you will reach the centre of the village and its minute church, again with a saddleback tower.

Turn right alongside the church and follow the cul-de-sac lane immediately on your left for ¼ mile to an isolated cottage. Beyond the cottage, an enclosed footpath continues to the right of a garage. Eventually this path enters an open field, where you follow the right-hand boundary alongside some woodland to a gate in the field's right-hand corner. Beyond this gate, you join the Daglingworth to Perrott's Brook road. Turn left and, in just 10 yards, cross a stone stile on the right-hand side into a field. Bear half-left across this field, following a line of three clearly visible stiles towards an avenue of trees in the distance. A short distance from the end of this avenue, cross a second stone stile and follow an enclosed path through the trees. In the next field, follow the left-hand field boundary alongside the woodland to the corner of the field and a stile. Cross to the opposite side of the next field, to an upright marker post and a stile 50 yards from the right-hand corner of the fence ahead. Beyond this stile, head half-right in the next field to a track and a second marker post and stile. Over this stile, head down the right-hand edge of the next two fields to a stile which leads into the grounds of Cirencester Golf Club. Pass to the left of the clubhouse and out onto the main A435 road. Over the last mile, you have descended from the hills above the Churn down into the valley itself.

Across the road from the clubhouse, follow an unmetalled lane until you see an old mill ahead. At this point, turn right onto a footpath which crosses the millstream by means of a wooden footbridge. This path enters an open field. Cross to a gateway on the far side, beyond which you cross a stream and turn left almost straightaway onto a well-defined bridlepath. This enclosed path follows a distinct route to the right of the stream for several hundred yards before entering a field. Pass through the handgate ahead, and continue along the bridlepath, at first along the foot of a field and later through some woodland. At the end of the woodland you reach the road at Perrott's Brook. Cross over and follow a lane past several large houses – names like Garden Cottage and Beech Wood should appear. Just beyond some overhead pylons, turn left onto an unmetalled drive that leads down to some farm buildings.

Follow what is effectively a bridlepath past these buildings and on past several cottages. The path passes to the right of the last cottage, before hitting open country and the last mile back to North Cerney. After an enclosed section that runs for some 200 yards, the path follows the bottom edge of an arable field with the fence to your left. At the end of this field, bear left into the next field and continue in the same direction, this time with the fence to the right. This open meadow gives you your first decent view of the Churn, just to your left. Some way across this field, pass through a gate on your right and continue following the field boundary northwards. Just as you approach North Cerney, you will see a large cottage on the left across the Churn. At this point, leave the valley bottom and bear uphill to the right to a stile in the wall ahead. Beyond is the road where you turn left to return to North Cerney and the Bathurst Arms. In the centre of the village, you will pass the village green and a rather fine lime tree. The inn is just a few yards down on the left-hand side.

54

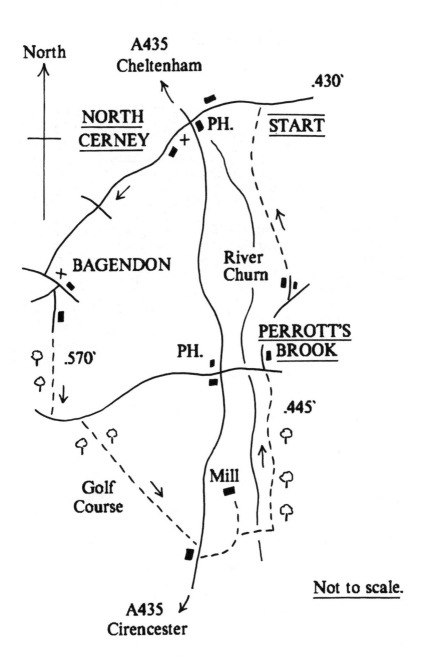

North

A435
Cheltenham

.430'

NORTH
CERNEY

PH.

START

BAGENDON

River
Churn

PERROTT'S
BROOK

PH.

.570'

.445'

Golf
Course

Mill

Not to scale.

A435
Cirencester

55

Coln St Aldwyns
The New Inn

The New Inn is a delightful building, constructed of the golden local stone and clad in ivy. With its stone-tiled roof, its pretty dormer windows and its very individual character, the residents of Coln St Aldwyns must have been absolutely delighted when the New Inn was granted a reprieve from threatened redevelopment. Internally, the main Courtyard Bar has a delightfully rural feel. The black beams and exposed stonework are complemented by a tiled floor overlain with a number of attractive rugs. The dry hops hanging from the ceiling provide a nice touch, whilst the mounted trout is wholly appropriate given the excellent fishing in the nearby Coln. The overall effect is completed by an iron cooking range at the far end of the bar. And if you fancy staying, there are eleven ensuite bedrooms.

The bar food at The New Inn offers an exceptional choice of home-cooked fare, with an extensive hand-written menu that changes daily. Old favourites such as soup of the day, ploughman's, steak and kidney pie and shepherd's pie are normally included – but beyond this there is always a lot more for the discerning palate, such as crispy duck and bacon salad, or poached red bream with char-grilled sweet peppers.

And how about a brandy snap basket filled with strawberries to follow? The beers available at the New Inn include the popular Hook Norton, brewed locally in a small Oxfordshire village, and the ever popular Wadworth 6X. There is outside seating in the courtyard, as well as seats and tables available at the front of the inn overlooking the quiet main street that runs through the village.

Telephone: (0285) 750651.

How to get there: Coln St Aldwyns lies 4 miles north of Fairford on an unclassified road. As you enter the village from nearby Quenington, the New Inn is on your right-hand side.

Parking: There is a car park through the archway at the far end of the courtyard. Ample roadside parking is also available nearby.

Length of the walk: 6 miles. Map: OS Landranger 163 Cheltenham and Cirencester (GR 146051).

Coln St Aldwyns is a delightful village, with its much restored church and stone cottages overlooking the clear waters of the Coln and the beech woods beyond. The river has reached these parts from the neighbouring village of Bibury, quite deservedly one of the most popular villages in the Cotswolds. Quintessentially English, Bibury is best typified by the much loved and photographed Arlington Row, a perfect rank of grey walled, grey roofed and gabled cottages that front onto a millstream that trickles down to the Coln. This undulating circuit explores these two villages, as well as the riverside meadows and hilltops that separate them. Although lacking the drama of the Cotswold escarpment further west, this is one of the most beautiful walks within the region.

The Walk

Turn left outside the New Inn and walk down through the village as far as the bridge across the river Coln. Just past this bridge, turn right alongside Yew Tree Lodge and follow the bridlepath that is signposted to the left of the beech woods ahead, veering away from the river. Cross the stile alongside the woods, and carry on uphill to a gate in the far left-hand corner of the field. Cross the next couple of fields, steering a course towards the house and barn in the distance. A gate at the far side of the second field brings you out onto an unmetalled drive. Cross this driveway and carry straight on to another gateway ahead, passing to the right of a complex of farm buildings. Cross the next field, aiming for the house in the left-hand corner. Just before you reach this house, a gate on the left takes you out onto the Quenington to Cirencester road.

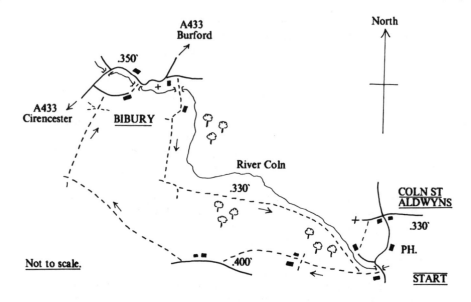

Turn right and, within 200 yards, right again onto a signposted footpath. This is in fact a well-defined track that will take you most of the way to Bibury. The path runs across the hilltops between Coln and Bibury, and brings with it far-ranging views across the local landscape. In about 1½ miles there is a crossroads of paths, with the housing on the outskirts of Bibury visible ahead. Turn right, follow the edge of the field to an intriguing five-fingered signpost, and continue straight on through a gateway and along an unmetalled road between some fine stone cottages. At the junction ahead, turn right, drop down the hill to pass in front of Arlington Row, and you reach the A433 in the centre of Bibury. I will leave you to explore the village at leisure, where one popular pastime is trout-spotting in the crystal clear waters of the Coln.

To continue, turn right along the A433, and follow this road for ¼ mile to the turning signposted to Coln St Aldwyns. Turn right along this turning and, in just 100 yards, right again onto a signposted bridlepath. After passing in front of the magnificent Bibury Court, now a hotel, the path crosses the Coln and winds its way through the buildings that make up Court Farm. Continue along this path, avoiding any tempting right-turns, with the Coln at the far side of the field on your left. Eventually, the path climbs a not insignificant rise before bearing to the left. Shortly it turns to the right, but our route continues straight ahead along a grassy track. Beyond a gateway, the path follows

58

the left-hand edge of the next field to a handgate, where the path descends to a stile. Aim for the left-hand edge of the wood ahead, where the path passes through a gate between the woods and the river Coln.

The next ½ mile is across delightful meadowland bordering the river. This is justifiably popular walking country, where thousands of pairs of boots have worn an obvious trail across the next few fields. Eventually, another area of woodland appears ahead. Make for the trees, keep to the left-hand edge of the wood and then cut through the far corner of the woodland onto one final open field. At the far side of this field lies Yew Tree Lodge and the road, where a left-turn returns you to the New Inn.

A short detour, though, will enable you to explore much of the village. Cross the Coln and turn immediately left along an access road that leads to a number of substantial houses. This road ends by a mill alongside a delightful millstream. Cross the waters by means of the footbridge, and follow the footpath on up the hill towards the church. Turn right along the road at the top of the path, having first explored the church, bear right when you reach the village store and the New Inn is just down the road on the left-hand side.

Southrop
The Swan

The Swan Inn, whose frontage is covered by a substantial creeper, stands in the centre of the village alongside a small green. Its simple furnishings – wooden tables and chairs, together with cottagey wall seats – help to maintain its traditional feel, as do the open fires that warm the bar during the winter months. The lounge is decorated with a mixture of prints and mirrors, hunting horns and tankards, whilst a 19th century advertisement announcing a timber sale in the village adds an element of historical interest. Exposed stonework and wooden beams add to the overall charm of the bar.

The Swan has developed a reputation for its food. All tastes appear to be catered for, with a typical lunchtime menu placing such staples as sausage and chips or cottage pie alongside such unusual selections as goat's cheese in puff pastry with cranberry sauce, or Stilton and onion soup! In addition to the normal menu, specials are chalked up in the bar. These might typically include curries, salmon and prawn pie or hot prawn and crab ramekin. In the evenings, the Swan has more of a restaurant feel, and has justifiably been awarded a rosette by the Good Pub Guide for its outstanding food.

Being a free house, the choice of beers and ales can change from time to time. A recent visit saw both Hook Norton and Morland Bitter on offer, both local beers from over the border in Oxfordshire. From further afield came Warsteiner, a German brew, produced using just spring water, hops, malt and yeast. The Swan also offers an excellent selection of wines. In addition to the expected Italian, German and French tipples, there are also a couple of Australian vintages available! These include the appropriately named Jacob's Creek, described as being 'dry red, soft and fruity'. The Swan deserves every success. Its imaginative food, the friendly and helpful service and the relaxed atmosphere, form the ideal mix of ingredients all pubs should have on offer.

Telephone: Southrop 205.

How to get there: Southrop lies 4 miles north-east of Fairford. An unclassified road leaves the A417 at the eastern end of Fairford and leads into the village. The Swan dominates the centre of the village, alongside the junction with the Eastleach Turville road.

Parking: There is ample room for careful roadside parking in the vicinity of The Swan.

Length of the walk: 4 ½ miles. Map: OS Landranger 163 Cheltenham and Cirencester (GR 201035).

The Leach is one of several Cotswold rivers that flow into Old Father Thames. Rising at Hampnett, just above Northleach, it flows south-eastwards to join the Thames at St John's Bridge near Lechlade. Just 3 miles upstream from Lechlade lies the small village of Southrop. Southrop borders the willows and watermeadows of the Leach, which forms the eastern boundary of the village.

To the west, the scarp slope of the Cotswolds overlooking the Severn Vale provides steep hillsides and dramatic views. To the east lies the dip slope, gently sloping landscape, undulating and perhaps less spectacular. It is this landscape that is explored in and around Southrop. This circular walk initially visits the open countryside to the west of the village, before descending into the neighbouring settlements of Eastleach Turville and Eastleach Martin. Here we find an archetypal Cotswold scene − the clear waters of the Leach crossed by a stone footbridge, daffodils in springtime, delightful churches and golden limestone cottages.

The return to Southrop follows the river Leach as closely as possible, with a few sections of actual riverbank walking. A suitable finale is the main street in Southrop where, after crossing the Leach, we pass water meadows, the local manor and a pleasing millhouse. A gentle, undemanding ramble, where the only warning that needs sounding is the possibility of sticky mud during the winter months.

North

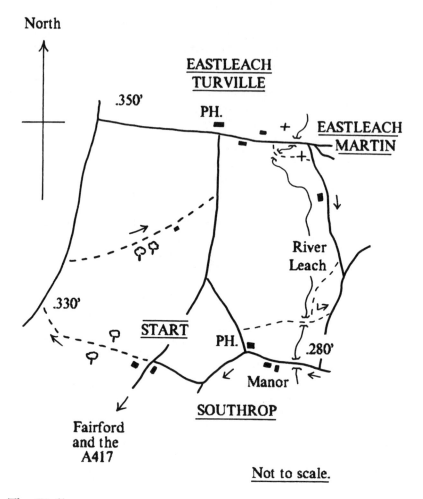

EASTLEACH
TURVILLE

.350'

PH.

EASTLEACH
MARTIN

River
Leach

.330'

START

PH.

.280'

Manor

SOUTHROP

Fairford
and the
A417

Not to scale.

The Walk

From The Swan, follow the Fairford road westwards out of the village
as far as the junction with the Eastleach road. Cross straight over at this
point, to follow a bridlepath that runs alongside a group of cottages.
The path initially takes on 'green lane' characteristics, before emerging
onto the open hilltop. The path now bears to the right and appears to
have a tarmac surface. This is in fact part of an old airfield that
occupied this flat hilltop during the Second World War, one of several
such sites dotted across the Cotswold plateau. Continue along the path
to a road.

62

Turn right, and follow the road for a short distance until it drops down into Hammersmith Bottom. At the foot of the hill, just before you cross a small stream – or dry stream bed! – turn right into a field and follow the bank of the stream for a few yards. Turn left into another field, and follow the left-hand hedgerow uphill through a couple of fields until you reach a hilltop copse. Continue along the grassy ride to the left of this copse, which becomes a farm track leading in ½ mile to the Eastleach Turville road.

Tun left, and in ¼ mile you descend into Eastleach Turville. On the hillside opposite is the imposing Victoria Inn, which is well worth visiting for its Arkell's beers. Follow the road to the right in front of the inn, signposted to Eastleach, and in 200 yards you will find yourself dropping downhill into Eastleach Martin. A picture-postcard prospect greets you. The Leach is crossed by a traditional stone footbridge, with the path on the far bank of the river leading to the picturesque St Martin's church. Follow this path in springtime, and a sea of golden daffodils will line your route. Having explored the sadly redundant St Martin's church, pass through the churchyard gate to the road beyond and turn right.

This lane leads back to Southrop, and borders the river Leach for much of its route. A ¼ mile out of Eastleach, you will pass a group of stone cottages and houses on the right. A few hundred yards on from this point, look out for the public footpath sign pointing the way into the trees on the right-hand side. The path leads down to the banks of the Leach, whose course is followed for 300 yards to another stone footbridge. You will in all probability disturb a rich variety of wildfowl with your progress. Rather than cross the footbridge, follow the track to the left to a small hamlet known as Fyfield. Turn right just past the first cottage to rejoin the Southrop road. In 200 yards, at the next junction, turn right to head back into Southrop village. This final stretch of the walk is pure delight, with the local manor, the river, water meadows and a rich variety of Cotswold architecture forming a suitable climax to the walk.

Cerney Wick
The Crown Inn

The Crown at Cerney Wick is located just to the east of the Cotswold Water Park, in the centre of a straggling village of stone cottages and farms. Just 200 yards to the rear of the inn lies the Thames and Severn Canal, although there are no apparent links between the hostelry and the one-time waterborne trade. The Crown is constructed of Cotswold stone, a building material that also provides a fine roofing material for the 17th century building. There are two cosy lounges, both decorated with an array of brasses. The main lounge contains an attractive fireplace which has been fitted-out with a wood burning stove. On the wall above the stove hangs a magnificent specimen of a deer's head. The other walls display a number of interesting bird prints, hung alongside several display cases of butterflies. Patio doors open onto a sunny, paved area with a number of picnic tables, alongside which is a children's play area.

The bar meals are the standard fare of ploughman's lunches, burgers, sausages, sandwiches, filled jacket potatoes and french fries, whilst the main menu contains a number of more tempting diversions. Starters could include deep fried crispy Camembert or breaded mushrooms, whilst the main courses include mariner's pie and steak and ale pie. To add to the calorific count, ice creams, fruit pies or fudge cake could complete your meal. Amongst the beers and ales on tap are Beamish Irish Stout and Courage Best, together with a most palatable Red Rock cider.

Telephone: Swindon 750369.

How to get there: Cerney Wick lies 5 miles south-east of Cirencester, just off the A419 Swindon road. As you follow the unclassified road into the village from the A419, the Crown is on your left-hand side.

Parking: There is a large car park to the rear of the Crown, which walkers patronising the inn can use.

Length of the walk: 3¾ miles. Map: OS Landranger 163 Cheltenham and Cirencester (GR 078959).

This is a flat, gentle excursion, with the main focus of attention created by a series of gravel pits known collectively as the Cotswold Water Park. The lakes extend over 1,500 acres, and offer a wide range of water sports and related activities. With the rich variety of wildfowl found on the waters, field glasses are a must. An added attraction is a short section of the long disused Thames and Severn Canal, that includes a couple of decaying locks and a finely restored lock-keeper's roundhouse.

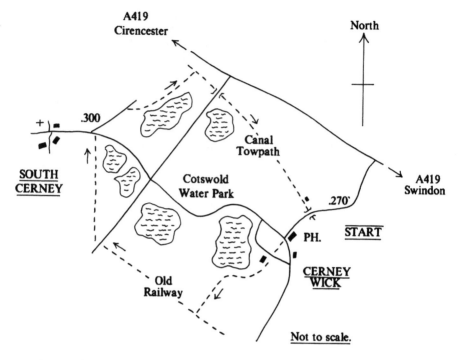

The Walk

Immediately opposite the Crown is a stile and a marker post reading 'Ashton Keynes 2m'. Cross this stile and follow the field-path across the field beyond to a second stile and a quiet lane. Cross a third stile the other side of this lane, and continue along the edge of the field beyond until you reach what is lake number 9 of the 75 lakes that make up the Cotswold Water Park. The wildfowl of these lakes is rich and varied, and includes grebes, herons, Canada geese, mute swans and red-crested pochard. Follow the perimeter of this lake for 400 yards or so to a point where the path bears to the right to pass between lake number 9 and lake number 71. At this point, bear to the left away from the lakeside to follow a waymarked path across a small footbridge and then along the left-hand side of a large field to reach a wide bridlepath. This is in fact the course of the old Cheltenham to Southampton railway – the Midland and South Western Junction – that closed in 1961. Its heyday was during the Second World War when it ferried thousands of troops to the South Coast as the Western armies assembled for D-Day. Follow the railway track bed to the right for ½ mile, cross the Water Park Spine Road, and continue along the track for another ½ mile until you join the South Cerney road. The mile of railway track walking will bring you glimpses of several other lakes in the area.

Turn to the left and follow the verge alongside the South Cerney road for 200 yards, before turning right into Wildmoorway Lane. A sign bears the legend 'Footpath Cerney Wick 1 ¾ miles'. Cross the old railway by means of the bridge ahead and, in just 100 yards, a stile on the right takes you off the lane and onto the bank of lake number 13. Follow the path alongside the lake as it runs parallel to Wildmoorway Lane, which you rejoin in ¼ mile. Take the footpath that continues in a north-easterly direction across the river Churn, signposted 'Public Footpath Information Layby'. Beyond the river, it continues as a wonderfully secluded enclosed path for almost ½ mile before joining the disused Thames and Severn Canal alongside the decaying Wilmoreway Lock. This waterway was cut in the late 18th century to link the Stroud valley with the Thames at Lechlade. West of Stroud, the Stroudwater Canal continued on to the Severn. The last through voyage on the T&S occurred in 1911, since when gentle decay has set in.

Turn right and follow the towpath for 1 mile back to Cerney Wick, crossing the Spine Road on your way. Just beyond the Spine Road, the towpath is a left-turn, whilst a right-turn would take you into the Information Layby. Back in Cerney Wick, the towpath passes the local lock and its adjoining roundhouse. These roundhouses were unique to the T&S, and were built between 1790 and 1794 to house the canal's lengthmen. Today they make rather attractive residences. Join the road leading to the Crown Inn, 200 yards to the right.

Coates
The Tunnel House Inn

Approached along a lonely unmetalled drive, the Tunnel House Inn is quite simply an isolated bow-fronted stone house surrounded by fields, grass and woodland. Once, 28 locks carried the Thames and Severn Canal from Stroud to its summit level, where a 3,817 yard tunnel pierced the Cotswold escarpment. Between 200 and 300 men, mainly West Country and Derbyshire miners, were employed digging out the Sapperton Tunnel, many of whom were accommodated in what is now the Tunnel House Inn. Today the inn stands like a sentry, guarding the finely restored eastern portal of the tunnel. Despite the valiant attempts of the Cotswold Canals Trust, the actual waterway appears to be in a quiet state of decay.

Internally, the inn's furnishings are quite unique, consisting of a totally random mixture of benches, window seats, uncoordinated armchairs, a sofa and vast wooden tables, all assembled in and around a traditional open fireplace. In winter, a blazing log fire warms the bar. This chaotic mix is complemented by any number of old maps, photographs, advertising signs, race tickets and goodness knows what else, displayed around the bar. The overall effect, however, is most pleasing. Unfortunately, Pythagoras the inn's pet python has outgrown its aquarium and departed to pastures new. Outside the inn are pleasant grassed areas surrounded by mature woodland, an excellent spot to pass an hour or two in high summer.

A range of good basic food is available at the Tunnel House Inn, running from ploughman's and burgers, through gala pie and cottage pie, to chicken in a barbecue sauce. Also on offer are tempting bacon or sausage butties. As well as Archers Best, Tetley and Wadworth 6X, this freehouse also offers Scrumpy Jack cider.

The Tunnel House Inn is perhaps my favourite Cotswold pub. The whole atmosphere of the place – its isolated location, its refusal to modernise or renovate, its unsophisticated food, its eccentric decor – is like no other pub in the area. I feel sure that if the 18th century canal navigators could return to Coates today, then they would feel perfectly at home. Long may the Tunnel House Inn continue to plough its own furrow!

Telephone: Cirencester 770280.

How to get there: The Tunnel House Inn lies off an unclassified lane running between Coates and Tarlton, 5 miles west of Cirencester. An unmetalled drive leads from the lane the ¼ mile to the inn.

Parking: There is a large parking area in front of the inn. There is also room for parking on the wide verges in the area.

Length of the walk: 3½ miles. Map: OS Landranger 163 Cheltenham and Cirencester (GR 965005).

This short, level circuit on the Cotswold plateau is full of interest. In addition to a unique inn, the disused Thames and Severn Canal and the eastern entrance to Sapperton Tunnel, the canal network's third longest tunnel, we also manage to fit in the official source of the river Thames at Thames Head. In between, there is an attractive stone village at Coates and a field-path that provides far-ranging views across the rolling countryside high on the hills. It really is surprising what you can unearth in a Cotswold backwater!

69

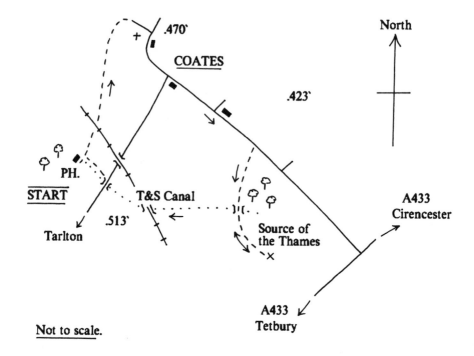

The Walk

From the inn, follow the drive across the top of the canal tunnel and cross the stile directly ahead into the adjoining field. At the far side of this field, the path drops down to cross the main London to Gloucester railway, before heading across a couple of fields to the village of Coates. The local landowner has left a grass strip across these fields to show the right of way. As you enter Coates, the path passes to the left of some farm buildings, before running alongside the churchyard to a road junction. Turn right at this junction and follow the road through the village for the next ½ mile, ignoring any left or right turns. Incidentally, if you make a detour to view the church you will find beyond the Norman doorway what has been described as 'a simple but most pleasing interior'.

A short distance ouside the village, just past the Coates name sign, cross the stile on the right-hand side and follow a signposted field-path. Keep the field boundary on the right-hand side until the path reaches another stile in the corner of the field. Cross this stile and turn left to follow a well-defined track down to Trewsbury Bridge and the bed of the Thames and Severn Canal. Cross the canal, pass through the gateway ahead and keep to the track as it passes through a couple of fields. Some way across a third field lies the source of Old Father Thames. The actual spot is on the left-hand side and is marked by a fine slab of granite, although water is rarely visible above ground.

Having paid suitable homage, retrace your steps to Trewsbury Bridge and descend to the canal towpath on the left-hand side. It is just over 1 mile along this derelict waterway to the entrance to Sapperton Tunnel and the adjoining Tunnel House Inn. Just after the canal passes under the London to Gloucester railway, you will discover a roundhouse on the left-hand side which was once the home of one of the lengthmen who worked on the canal. The canal passes through a wooded cutting on its final approach to Sapperton Tunnel, whilst a path climbs the left-hand side of the tunnel entrance to reach the inn.

Sapperton
The Daneway

The Daneway is an excellent Cotswold inn, tucked away in an isolated wooded valley seemingly a million miles away from the present day. The late 18th century was a time of great activity in the Golden Valley above Stroud. Work on the Thames and Severn Canal was progressing apace, with the major engineering project to be completed being the 3,817 yard long Sapperton Tunnel that pierced the Cotswold plateau. A lodging house was built at the western approach to the tunnel to house the West Country and Derbyshire miners employed on the project, and it was this lodging house that later became the Daneway Inn. It subsequently served as a watering hole to the bargees whose thirsts needed quenching after the ordeal of 'legging' through the nearby tunnel. Today the inn sits overlooking the derelict and overgrown waterway, a whitewashed building with a fine Cotswold stone roof. The harnesses and brasses in the lounge are a testimony to the days of the towing horses.

The traditionally furnished lounge bar is dominated by a quite remarkable fireplace, with its carved oak decorations running from the floor to the ceiling. There is also a public bar, a small family room and an attractive garden that slopes down to the former canal bed. The range of food is as traditional as the inn itself – filled rolls, baked potatoes and ploughman's – although wider tastes are catered for by such interesting diversions as beef and Guinness pie, vegetable gratin and hot smoked mackerel. The sweets include chocolate fudge cake, apple pie and cream and banana split. Real ale drinkers are well catered for, with both Archers and Badger Bitter on tap, as well as the locally brewed Daneway Bitter. Quite simply, a superb Cotswold pub in a most picturesque setting that I for one never tire of visiting. Telephone: (0285) 760297.

How to get there: The Daneway Inn lies just below Sapperton village in a rather quiet corner of the Cotswolds. Sapperton is signposted from the A419 Cirencester to Stroud road, whilst in the village you follow the minor road signposted to Edgeworth and Bisley. This passes the Daneway.

Parking: There is a large car park for patrons in front of the Daneway Inn, with little further scope for parking on the narrow lanes in the vicinity.

Length of the walk: 3 miles. Map: OS Landranger 163 Cheltenham and Cirencester (GR 939034).

This short walk explores the upper Frome valley, high above Stroud, where we find the decaying remains of the Thames and Severn Canal piercing the Cotswold plateau by means of the Sapperton Tunnel. This is an area of steep-sided wooded valleys, quite beautiful in autumn months. Just occasionally, a view is afforded of the locality from some isolated vantage point, and quite dramatic and far-ranging these views turn out to be. Lovers of Cotswold architecture will find a great deal to behold in the small village of Sapperton. St Kenhelm's church, with its Jacobean woodwork and stone monuments, is an absolute gem. An excellent ramble in a corner of the Cotswolds that is justifiably popular with walkers.

The Walk
Cross the road alongside the Daneway Inn and follow the footpath opposite signposted to Chalford. This overgrown right of way is in fact the towpath of the long disused Thames and Severn Canal, as is soon evident from the decaying lock chambers that begin to appear. In less than ½ mile, the towpath switches to the south bank of the waterway by means of a wooden footbridge, and in a similar distance you will reach a stone and brick bridge over the canal bed. Cross this bridge, and straight ahead you will see the entrance to Siccaridge

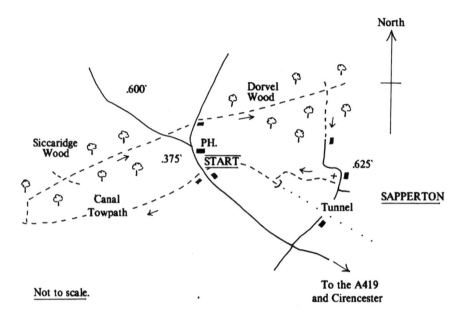

North

.600'

Dorvel Wood

Siccaridge Wood

PH.

.375' START

.625'

SAPPERTON

Canal Towpath

· Tunnel

Not to scale.

To the A419 and Cirencester

Wood Nature Reserve, a delight for lovers of traditional English flora. Just as you enter the wood, take the left-hand fork uphill, and in just a matter of yards bear right at another fork. The path continues climbing through the woodland until it reaches a clearing where a cross-track cuts across the right of way. Head straight across and continue following the main path through the wood for ½ mile until you join the Sapperton to Edgeworth lane. A right-turn here would give you a premature return to the Daneway, and is an excellent short cut if the heavens open!

The main walk continues by crossing the lane and the stile opposite into an open field, where you follow a course through a shallow valley for ¼ mile. The slopes on either side are pitted with rabbit burrows, and a sharp eye will quickly detect a disappearing tail. The field-path eventually bears to the left to descend to Dane Lane, where you turn left and almost immediately right onto a stony track that climbs the hillside into Dorvel Wood. In just a matter of yards, ignore an indistinct left fork and continue along the main track through the woodland. There is a second fork in a few hundred yards, where you bear to the left, and continue along the woodland path for a further ½ mile to a point where a smaller path crosses the main track. Turn right, and descend a quite steep and potentially muddy slope, heading straight across at the cross-track reached in just 50 yards. Just before

74

the valley bottom, fork left and continue uphill passing a marvellously secluded stone cottage on the left-hand side. When you join the access road to this cottage, turn right and continue uphill into Sapperton village.

Turn right into the churchyard of St Kenhelm's church, where it is worth spending some time exploring this fine ecclesiastical building. The quite magnificent woodwork inside St Kenhelm's was transferred from the local manor house which was demolished in 1730, whilst the stone monuments which will also catch your eye are of Sir Henry Poole and his family (1616) and Sir Robert Atkyns (1711). Bear left at the church porch and follow the path out through a kissing-gate and onto another footpath. Turn right and, in a few yards, you will emerge into an open field that affords a quite spectacular view down into the Frome valley. Bear sharp left and follow the fence along the top of this bumpy field for 100 yards until you reach a stile on the left. At this point, head half-right down the hillside to a stile into the trees some 200 yards distant. Beyond the stile, the path crosses the top of the western portal of the Sapperton Tunnel, before dropping down to the towpath alongside the derelict Tunnel Cottage. It is just ½ mile of pleasant towpath walking back to the Daneway Inn, where a glass of the locally brewed Daneway Bitter should be high on your list of priorities!

Cranham
The Royal William

The history of the Royal William can but be a matter of speculation. During the heyday of the coaching era, both the Bath to Gloucester and the Chippenham to Worcester cross roads passed the Royal William, although the inn is not listed as a stopping point in Cary's 1821 'Itinerary of the Great Roads'. Maybe the name is derived from a surprise visit from a passing Royal!

Today's Royal William is one of Whitbread's 'Brewers Fayre' inns. There is one large central bar that serves both the lounge and the adjoining family room. The decor and furnishings are essentially reproduction – prints, shelving units, lamps, beams and tables all matching the chain's nationwide design and style. Despite this lack of originality, however, the Royal William presents a relaxed and comfortable setting in which to enjoy refreshment. The Royal William has a good selection of ales on tap that range from Whitbread's own Flowers Original and IPA, to Boddingtons, Marston's and Murphy's Stout. A pleasant, if unsurprising, inn that will provide welcome sustenance at the end of a fine Cotswold ramble.

Telephone: Painswick 813650.

How to get there: The Royal William lies on the A46 Stroud to Cheltenham road, 3 miles to the north of Painswick.

Parking: There is a parking bay on the A46 opposite the Royal William, as well as a large car park for patrons to the rear of the inn.

Length of the walk: 5 miles. Map: OS Landranger 162 Gloucester and the Forest of Dean (GR 878127).

This walk encapsulates the very best of the Cotswolds – high hilltops, remote valleys, a traditional woollen town and isolated dwellings that include a mill and a court. From the Royal William, the circuit crosses Painswick Hill to reach the town of Painswick itself. This is an elegant settlement, made wealthy by the woollen trade of the 17th and 18th centuries. Its most noted attraction is the churchyard of St Mary's church, where the number of yew trees is said to toal 99 – all attempts to establish yew number 100 have ended in failure! The return is by way of the picturesque Painswick valley, where your steps will pass Damsell's Mill and Tocknell's Court before the stiff climb back to the Royal William. The Court is well over 300 years old, and sits beautifully amidst delightful gardens and grounds alongside the lcoal stream.

The Walk
The walk begins by following the lane uphill alongside the Royal William inn. In about 250 yards, at a junction of paths, fork to the right to follow the Cotswold Way signs. These are a combination of white circles and coloured arrows which, in fact, waymark the route into Painswick. The clear path continues across various golf fairways for ¾ mile before joining an unclassified lane. Incidentally, the bumpy ground on the right is a hillfort and marks the site of Painswick Beacon. It is worth making the necessary detour to the trig point to enjoy the fine views across the Severn Vale towards Cheltenham and Gloucester. Turn left at the road and, in a short distance, right along the waymarked Cotswold Way as it passes alongside Catsbrain Quarry. The local stone is a valuable commodity which one drystone wall builder informed me sells for £36 a ton! Beyond the quarry, the path descends through some secluded woodland before joining another golf fairway. Cross this fairway and continue following a path that runs alongside a cemetery wall. Where the wall ends, there is yet another golf fairway to cross, beyond which the Cotswold Way crosses another unclassified lane and passes through some woodland to join yet another minor road. Turn right at this point, and left when you join the B4073 that leads into Painswick.

As you come into the town, continue straight ahead down Gloucester Road, ignoring the 'No Entry' sign, and in just 400 yards you will join the busy A46. At this point, you will perhaps wish to explore 'Painswick Proud'. I will leave you to seek out the parish church, the 99 yews, the table tombs and much elegant architecture besides! The Tourist Information Centre is 200 yards to the right along the A46, in the local library, if you want further information.

To return to the Royal William, cross the A46 into Bisley Street and, just past an old chapel, turn left into Vicarage Street. In 200 yards, a lane to Sheepscombe forks off to the right, whilst we continue on for just a few yards to Museum Cottage and a farm track on the right-hand side. Follow this bridlepath for close on ½ mile through to Highgrove House (not THE Highgrove House!) where Painswick is very clearly left behind and we are in the heart of the delightfully rural Painswick valley. The path continues to the right of the house and is followed directly across a couple of fields to a footbridge across the Painswick stream. Route finding is very straightforward hereabouts due to an excellent network of stiles and marker posts. Cross the stream and turn immediately to the left to follow its east bank for ½ mile through to Damsell's Mill. This is a delightfully secluded woodland path where the ground is awash with a carpet of flowers in springtime.

Cross the road alongside the mill, cross the stile opposite and follow the field-path directly alongside the stream through two fields to a stile into a small patch of woodland. Follow the only path through these trees, cross the stream just below a point where its waters tumble through a decaying archway and bear right to continue along the path as it passes in front of a lonely and isolated farm cottage. Just 25 yards past this cottage, cross a stile on the left-hand side and continue across the fields to Tocknell's Court. From the Court, you can either follow the driveway through to the Cranham road or cross the stream to follow a recently opened permissive path that runs parallel to the drive but on the opposite bank of the river. This is the better option since the path passes through a traditionally managed wildflower meadow.

At the road, turn left for a steep climb back to the Royal William. The road as shown on the OS sheet is marked with one of those black arrows that signify that puffing and panting is in order! About 100 yards before you join the A46, leave the road and bear left along a path leading into the trees. This provides a pleasant short cut back to the Royal William, obviating the need for an unpleasant 150 yards of A46 walking. After the steep climb of something like 250 ft in the ½ mile up from Tocknell's Court, the pint of Boddingtons awaiting you at the inn will prove something of a necessity!

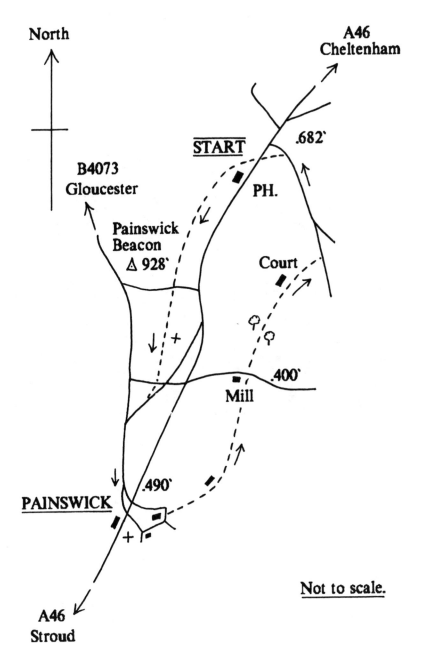

North

A46
Cheltenham

START

.682`

B4073
Gloucester

PH.

Painswick
Beacon
△ 928`

Court

.400`
Mill

PAINSWICK

.490`

Not to scale.

A46
Stroud

79

Minchinhampton Common
The Old Lodge Inn

The Old Lodge Inn, originally a 16th century hunting lodge, lies at the western end of Minchinhampton Common, perched above the Nailsworth valley. Externally, the Old Lodge is a rather unpretentious stone building with a pleasant walled garden. The walls, unfortunately, severely restrict the inn's view of the surrounding area! Inside the Old Lodge are a number of bars – a lounge bar, Tom Long's bar, a restaurant, a family room and a games room. Even well-controlled dogs are welcome. The main bars and the restaurant are based around a central serving area, with each room revealing a wealth of exposed beams and stonework. The walls are decorated with a number of prints and items of brasswork. The impressive fox head that adorns the bar is perhaps indicative of the inn's history. With comfortable sofas, low ceilings and tasteful lighting, the Old Lodge presents a cosy, intimate atmosphere.

The range of bar food is vast and is displayed on blackboards inside the inn. The usual categories – starters, ploughman's, salads and sandwiches – are available, well over 140 different bar meals. These include sizzle meals, vegetarian meals and Yorkshire pudding meals. Two thoroughly recommended options are the steak and Guinness pie and the wild boar pie. Served in large oval dishes, these pies are a meal in themselves even without vegetables and potatoes. The wild boar pie, incidentally, contains cider, slices of venison and vegetables. The choice of beers and ales at this freehouse is equally varied. Wadworth 6X, Theakston, Old Spot and Speckled Hen are all on tap, whilst both Copperhead and Old English ciders are available.

The Old Lodge does lie a little off the beaten track, from the outside the building might appear a little rundown and the entrance might be in need of a little signposting, but this is more than compensated for by the sheer variety of food and drink that is available in most relaxed and comfortable surroundings. A pub well worth seeking out. Tom Long, incidentally, was a local highwayman who committed suicide rather than face capture. Tom Long's Post on the common, where a number of roads meet, marks his burial spot.

Telephone: Stroud 832047.

How to get there: The Old Lodge Inn lies on Minchinhampton Common, 1 ½ miles west of Minchinhampton, just off the unclassified road to Amberley. The inn lies alongside the locally signposted golf club.

Parking: Parking for the Old Lodge is available on the common alongside the inn.

Length of the walk: 4 ½ miles. Map: OS Landranger 162 Gloucester and the Forest of Dean (GR 854008).

Minchinhampton Common is a high level plateau surrounded by fine valleys – the Frome valley to the north, the Nailsworth valley to the south-west. Its 580 acres, used for sheep grazing since time immemorial, are now a National Trust property. This circular ramble around the edges of the common brings fine views without the slightest hint of a steep climb – just the scenario most walkers must dream of! Being common land, there are no actual footpaths, only landmarks to aim for. With this in mind, a clear fine day is not only necessary for the view but also for route finding. In misty or foggy weather, it would be quite easy to end up well and truly lost!

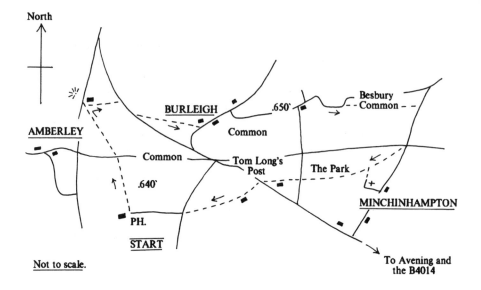

North

AMBERLEY

BURLEIGH

.650'

Common

Besbury
Common

Common

Tom Long's
Post

The Park

.640'

MINCHINHAMPTON

PH.

START

Not to scale.

To Avening and
the B4014

The Walk

From the Old Lodge, head northwards across the common towards the right-hand edge of the houses some ½ mile distant. En route, you will cross the Amberley to Minchinhampton road, and you might well have to dodge low-flying golf balls! Just before you reach a second road on the edge of Amberley, turn right to follow the boundary wall of a house . . . unless you wish to make a detour across the road to a war memorial on the edge of the common from where fine views of the Stroud valley can be obtained.

Where the boundary wall ends, continue across the common, bearing slightly to the right until you reach another road. This will involve dropping down into an old quarry depression. Turn right at the road and follow its grassy edge for 150 yards past another disused quarry depression. Beyond this point, bear to the left away from the road across the common to the next road, which leads into the village of Burleigh. Walk through the village until, just past a telephone box, you turn right into Burleigh Lane. This is a classic example of the English country lane – stone walls, high on the hillside, with constant views to the north into the Frome valley.

In almost ½ mile, continue straight on at a point where a road joins from the right to shortly bear off on the left. This complex sounding procedure takes place in front of Burleigh House. In another ¼ mile, fork left at a junction alongside a signpost bearing the legend Love

82

Lane. I am sure that place-name experts can explain this one! Continue along Love Lane for a few hundred yards until you turn off onto the NT's Besbury Common property on your right-hand side. Follow the footpath along the edge of this common for ¼ mile or so, enjoying the extensive views to the north of the Frome valley. When this path meets a quiet country lane, turn right to head into Minchinhampton. In ¼ mile, you will reach a crossroads. The road ahead goes into Minchinhampton – which you may care to explore – whilst across the junction to the right lies the NT's Great Park, and our return path to the Old Lodge.

Head half-right across the Great Park to the stone wall some 400 yards ahead, and continue following this wall to the right until you reach two substantial properties – Seymour House and Westfield. The embankment that parallels much of your route is the Bulwarks, the remains of an Iron Age hillfort that defended this high plateau. Just beyond Westfield, where the stone wall bears sharply to the left, continue across the open common to another pair of substantial properties a couple of hundred yards ahead, surrounded by a clump of Scots pine trees and another stone wall. Follow this wall to the right, past Windmill House, and some 600 yards ahead the Old Lodge Inn comes into view. Make your way back across the common to the inn.

Uley
The Old Crown

The Old Crown enjoys a picturesque location alongside the local village green and opposite St Giles' church. All around are handsome Cotswold stone properties, overlooked by Uley Hill and its vast hillfort. The Old Crown is constructed of the local stone and fronts onto the B4066 Dursley to Stroud road. The pub is divided into a lounge/dining area, bar and a darts/children's room. A number of exposed beams lend character to the inn, and support a collection of tankards as well as the ceiling, whilst on the walls are displayed some interesting photographs and prints. These include shots of the local football team when proud winners of the Berkeley Hospital Cup, local village scenes from ages past and pictogram maps of the village and its environs. There is, quite naturally, the almost obligatory brasswork. To the rear of the inn is a sun-trap of a beer garden, containing a number of picnic tables.

This is a freehouse with Boddingtons and Whitbread PA on tap, but a more interesting beer is that brewed locally at the Uley Brewery. The prize winning Uley Bitter and Uley Old Spot beers are truly excellent, and make this pub well worth a visit. A good range of bar food is available – specials, sandwiches, jacket potatoes, ploughman's, grills, sweets and children's food. The prices are very reasonable and the helpings quite substantial. The more unusual offerings include smoked haddock tagliatelle and vegetable provençal, whilst the ploughman's include the normal Stilton and Cheddar varieties, together with the novel Lincolnshire sausage alternative. If you can manage a sweet, there are the ever-popular apple pies, cherry pies and apricot crumbles, spotted dick and chocolate sponge.

The Old Crown is a welcoming and unpretentious inn. A solid and dependable Cotswold pub that is worthy of your custom.

Telephone: Dursley 860502.

How to get there: The Old Crown lies at the northern end of the village of Uley, opposite the church, on the B4066 Dursley to Stroud road.

Parking: The Old Crown has a car park at the rear. There is also ample room for careful roadside parking along the B4066.

Length of the walk: 2 miles. Map: OS Landranger 162 Gloucester and the Forest of Dean (GR 792986).

Uley lies at the head of the Cam valley, surrounded on all sides by steep hillsides and slopes. The Old Crown is the starting point for this short ramble that climbs onto Uley Hill, the site of the finest hillfort in the Cotswolds. The 1 mile of ramparts bring exceptional views across the Severn Vale to the distant Welsh Hills.

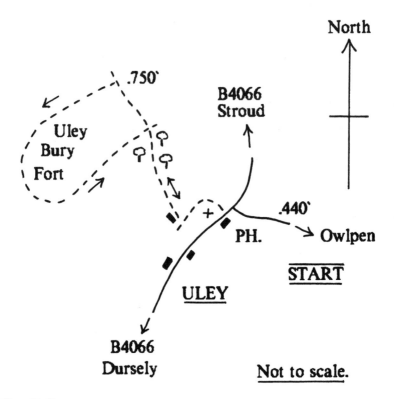

The Walk

Cross the road alongside the Old Crown and follow the footpath that passes behind the village church. This path is signposted as leading to Uley Bury and Whitecourt. At the rear of the church, the path forks alongside a bungalow named Hillcroft. Turn right and follow a short enclosed path to a stile and an open field. The view awaiting you will be somewhat daunting – a 350 ft climb onto the ramparts of Uley Bury hillfort in just 400 yards . . . probably a gradient not far short of 1-in-3! Head straight up the hillside to the edge of the woodland ahead, and follow the perimeter of the woodland to the left until you reach a handgate within 200 yards. Beyond this gateway, continue along the clear woodland path that continues climbing the hill to the left. This fine deciduous woodland is richly blessed with flora in the spring and early summer – anemones, wild garlic, bluebells, celandine and any number of traditional wild flowers. At the top of the woodland path, a handgate brings you to the eastern corner of Uley Bury. The ramparts are directly opposite.

86

Follow the footpath ahead that leads along the north-eastern rampart, fine views on your right of the upper Cam valley. A small parking area marks the northern tip of the hillfort. Here the path bears to the left to follow the north-western side of Uley Bury. The views are now dominated by Cam Long Down and the distant river Severn. The path eventually bears to the left to continue along the south-western ramparts, with Downham Hill, Dursley and the distant North Nibley Monument now the dominant landmarks. Finally, the path bears to the left to follow the south-eastern edge of the hillfort, Uley village spread out below along the valley bottom. Eventually the perimeter path returns to the north-eastern rampart, and a right-turn brings you back to the woodland stile leading back into the woodland walked through earlier. It is now simply a question of retracing your steps to Uley church and the Old Crown, only this time around it is all downhill!

Kingscote
Hunters Hall

Hunters Hall is on the busy A4135 just to the west of the village of Kingscote, and has held a continuous licence for over 500 years. Passing custom has always been important to the inn, whether it be today's commercial travellers and holiday-makers, or the coaches that travelled England's byways in centuries past. Cary's 'Itinerary of the Great Roads' lists Kingscote as being on the Bath to Birmingham coaching route, a service that passed Colonel Kingscote's seat deep in rural Gloucestershire. This might explain the reference to hunting in the inn's name. Certainly this creeper-covered building conveys a great sense of history.

Internally, there is no shortage of space. As well as the usual public bar and lounge bar, there is a food serving and eating area, a back room with its pool table and darts board and an upstairs gallery reserved for eating purposes. If all of this isn't enough, there is also a large beer garden with an extensive children's play area. Hunters Hall is furnished in a suitably traditional manner – in addition to the flagstones, exposed stone walls, beams and open fireplaces, there are easy chairs, sofas, sturdy settles and oak tables.

Hunters Hall offers an extensive range of bar snacks and meals. In addition to the usual sandwiches, ploughman's and rolls, there is an ever-changing choice of special dishes chalked up in the eating area. A recent visit saw French onion soup, garlic bread, smoked trout pate and goat's cheese with spice and pepper on offer for starters. The main dishes included duck and orange pie, pork steak grilled with bacon and cheese, lamb and mushroom curry, barbecued chicken wings and savoury beef crumble. Each meal was accompanied by an excellent choice of salads available from a self-service bar. Children are well catered for with their own menu that includes old favourites like beefburgers, sausage, fish fingers and chicken nuggets, all served with the obligatory chips and baked beans. Being a freehouse, there is a good range of beers and ales available. These include Bass, Hook Norton and Smiles, as well as the excellent Old Spot brew from the local Uley Brewery.

Telephone: Dursley 860393.

How to get there: Hunters Hall lies on the A4135 Dursley to Tetbury road, 4 miles east of Dursley.

Parking: There is a large car park to the rear of the inn. Alternatively, there is room for careful roadside parking on the minor road opposite the inn that leads into Kingscote village.

Length of the walk: 5½ miles. Map: OS Landranger 162 Gloucester and the Forest of Dean (GR 814960). This fine ramble is a relatively complicated walk to describe, with many field and woodland paths where the right of way is neither distinct nor clearly waymarked. I would thoroughly recommend that you obtain a copy of the relevant OS 1:25 000 Pathfinder Sheet (1133), and do some preparatory homework prior to the walk.

Kingscote and Hunters Hall lie high on the Cotswold plateau, sitting astride the 700 ft contour line. To the east of Kingscote, however, this level landscape gives way to the Cotswold escarpment and its associated valleys in and around Wotton-under-Edge and Dursley. This walk explores a number of these marvellously secluded valleys, whose steep sides and damp marshy bottoms have prevented the march of the plough and its associated arable crops. Lengthy sections of this walk follow the tributary valleys that feed into Ozleworth Bottom. The dense woodland cover and the streams that follow the valley floors mean that the going is inevitably muddy and damp, other than during a prolonged heatwave. This, combined with the dense undergrowth, means that suitable clothing and footwear are important on this ramble. If you are tempted to wear trainers and shorts, then be prepared for damp feet and nettle stings!

The Walk

Take the unclassified lane that runs alongside Hunters Hall signposted to Bagpath. Follow this lane south-eastwards for ¾ mile to a junction where a right-turn is signposted to Uley and Dursley. Ignore this turning, instead turn right along a second lane that appears in just 20 yards. Almost immediately, you will see a bridlepath signposted on the left-hand side. Follow the bridlepath for 100 yards to a gateway, continue through a second gateway some 20 yards ahead, and bear right across the field ahead. There is no obvious path, but your target is the valley bottom where a small stream lies hidden amongst a jungle of trees, bushes and general undergrowth. Continue following this well hidden stream southwards for the next ½ mile along an area of scrubland, the sound of running water to your right and dense woodland to your left. Eventually, the path passes through a gateway into a wide open field that fills the valley bottom. The stream now comes out into the open and the whole valley opens up to provide a marvellous vista. Continue following the stream southwards for another ¾ mile, always keeping to the left-hand bank a few yards above the waterway.

Eventually, the valley forms a junction with a second valley running east to west. This is in fact the upper part of Ozleworth Bottom. At the 'junction', bear left and follow another small stream eastwards into some dense woodland. Again, the stream is initially well hidden in the undergrowth, but it flows along what is clearly the valley bottom. For the next 1½ miles, literally follow the one-and-only footpath through the damp marshy woodland, your steps running parallel to this stream which occasionally criss-crosses the right of way. About ¾ mile into the woods, you will cross a fairly conspicuous downhill track, whilst in another ¾ mile you will leave the tree cover by way of an old metal gate to emerge into an open field. The appearance of daylight and open skies actually comes as something of a welcome relief after the nearest thing that the Cotswolds can offer to primeval jungle!

Head straight across this field, until you see the imposing residence that dominates Lasborough Park come into view on the left-hand side. Just past the house, bear left to cross the driveway and climb the hillside ahead bearing half-right all the while. In ½ mile, in the far northern boundary wall of the Lasborough Park grounds, you will find a small handgate. It is a short distance down the wall from the main gateway in the corner of the field. Beyond this handgate, a field-path high above the valley brings you to the remains of a small Norman castle – the ditch around the mound would have been the moat. The views hereabouts are especially impressive. From the hilltop vantage point, the tiny hamlet of Newington Bagpath lies below in the valley,

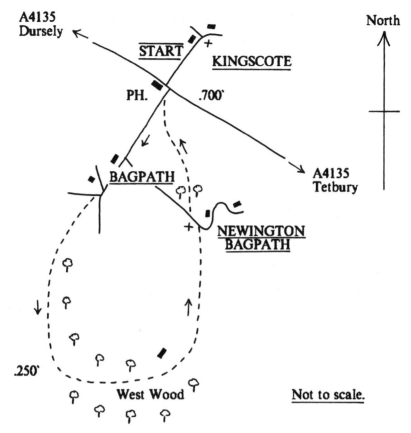

A4135
Dursely

START

KINGSCOTE

PH.   .700'

BAGPATH

A4135
Tetbury

NEWINGTON
BAGPATH

.250'

West Wood   Not to scale.

whilst the impressive complex of buildings on the far side of the valley a little way back were Lasborough Manor and its adjoining Victorian church. Just beyond the ancient motte, pass out onto the lane that leads down to Newington Bagpath. On your left is the redundant parish church.

Turn left along the lane and, in just a few yards, go through a gateway on the right-hand side. Follow the path that runs alongside the right-hand boundary wall until you reach an area of woodland. Continue through this woodland, keeping left at one fork, until the path emerges into a sheep pasture at the foot of a hillside. Turn left and follow the edge of the field until you reach a gateway, beyond which a track heads uphill into the trees. Continue following this path, as it follows the field boundaries of the next couple of fields, before emerging alongside Hunters Hall.

Waterley Bottom
The New Inn

Waterley Bottom, a secluded Cotswold valley a mile or two east of
North Nibley, is the home of one of the area's most isolated pubs. As
if the name Waterley Bottom were not enough, directions that talk of
steep hills with 1-in-5 gradients might deter all but the most intrepid
of visitors! In fact, this is not the case, with the New Inn having earned
itself a proud reputation for its wide selection of real ales and its good
value food. In fact, it has recently been voted *Pub of the Year (south-west
region)* by CAMRA.

The inn is located at the end of a cul-de-sac lane, reached via a
complex network of country byways. True to its name, the New Inn
does not appear to be a building of any great antiquity. Indeed, its
plaster-rendered walls and modern-tiled roof could well make it the
creation of 20th century man. Internally, the inn houses a public bar
and a lounge. The public bar is simply furnished with modern tables
and chairs, although one or two bench seats add an element of
contrast. The wood-panelled walls, decorated with various livestock
prints, complete the public bar, where a darts board and trophy
cabinet suggest that many a fierce-fought match has occurred within
its confines! The lounge is comfortably furnished with cushioned
chairs and high-backed settles, with exposed stonework reminding

visitors that this is Cotswold country. The windows in the lounge look out onto the inn's garden, with the open countryside beyond.

The New Inn is a freehouse, and has develolped a reputation for its wide selection of beers and ales. These might typically include Cotleigh Tawny, Greene King Abbot, Smiles Best and Theakston Old Peculier. An unusual offering was Inch's cider, not a brew that pops up in too many pubs. The New Inn offers traditional pub food at value for money prices.

Telephone: Dursley 543659.

How to get there: The New Inn offers limited parking possibilities for walkers. This walk, therefore, begins at Wotton-under-Edge, with the inn forming a refreshment stop en route. This also reduces the chance of your car having a bump on the narrow lanes around Waterley Bottom! Allow approximately 1½ hours to reach the New Inn from Wotton – a mid-morning start should see you reach the inn for lunch.

Parking: Wotton-under-Edge lies on the junction of the B4058 Bristol to Nailsworth road, and the B4060 Chipping Sodbury to Cam road. In the centre of the town, park alongside St Mary the Virgin church, a few yards along the B4058 from the town's war memorial.

Length of the walk: 6 miles. Map: OS Landranger 162 Gloucester and the Forest of Dean (GR 760934).

Wotton-under-Edge – the village in the wood – developed as a woollen centre in medieval times. The town was a thriving weaving and spinning centre, a fact that is still reflected by the presence of sheep and teasels on the town's arms. The Cotswold Edge rises steeply above the town, dominated by Wotton Hill, a local viewpoint that brings panoramic views across Wotton and its environs. Two miles north-east of Wotton, nestled at the foot of the hills, lies the village of North Nibley. Standing aloft on the hilltop above Nibley is the Tyndale Monument, a vast stone edifice erected to commemorate William Tyndale. Theological students will remember Tyndale as the translator of the first English Bible, and he at one time resided in the area.

This strenuous walk explores these various themes. From Wotton, a steep climb takes us onto the hilltops, before a secluded valley is followed downhill through to the New Inn at Waterley Bottom. From the inn, another stiff climb brings us to the Tyndale Monument and with it expansive views across the Severn Vale. A section of the Cotswold Way is then followed back to Wotton, taking in Westridge Wood and Wotton Hill. The outward leg of the walk is mainly on quiet lanes and byways, where little traffic is likely to be encountered.

The Walk

The walk begins outside St Mary the Virgin church in Wotton, where a fine Perpendicular tower and the late 14th century brass of Lord and Lady Berkeley will certainly catch your eye. About 150 yards along the B4058 from the church, turn left into Adeys Lane. Climb this steep lane for almost ½ mile, before turning right onto a waymarked footpath immediately before a detached house. The path climbs the hillside behind this house, up through a delightful beech wood, before

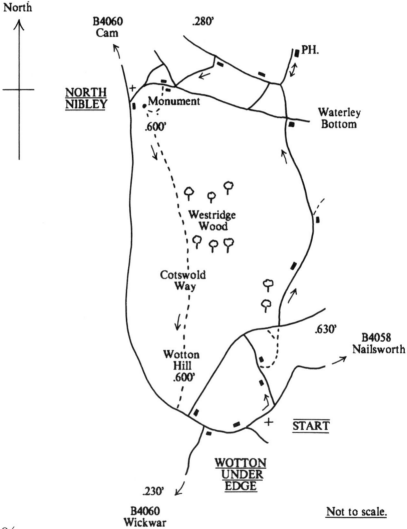

North

B4060
Cam

.280'

PH.

NORTH
NIBLEY

Monument

Waterley
Bottom

.600'

Westridge
Wood

Cotswold
Way

.630'

B4058
Nailsworth

Wotton
Hill
.600'

START

WOTTON
UNDER
EDGE

.230'

B4060
Wickwar

Not to scale.

reaching a junction at the top of the climb. Whilst pausing for breath at this point, admire the views back across the town. Turn left at the junction and, in a matter of yards, bear to the right at a distinct fork. The path emerges onto a quiet lane.

Follow the turning opposite signposted to Waterley Bottom. For the next few hundred yards, this lane descends through woodland before emerging into a secluded valley. Continue along this lane for 1 mile, to a crossroads. Head straight across, following the Dursley turning, and in 200 yards turn right to reach the New Inn.

Suitably refreshed, retrace your steps down the lane from the inn. Ignore the first left-turn, our inward route, instead continue ahead along the lane to Wotton and Dursley. In a few yards, fork right at a junction and continue along the road ahead for ½ mile until you reach an old farm. This road passes along the hillside, above the valley on your left, with fine views stretching away to the Cotswold Edge above Nibley.

Take a left turn just beyond the farm, and follow the lane down past a row of whitewashed cottages and uphill through a small hamlet to a junction. Here you will find a phone box on a small green. Take the right-hand turning, signposted to North Nibley and marked with a 'road narrows' sign. Continue along this road for just under ½ mile until a footpath is marked on the left, just past a detached house. Turn left at this point, and follow the left-hand field boundary beyond up the hillside onto the high wolds. The steep climb eventually brings you into woodland, where you keep following the main path until you reach a stile at the top of the hill. Cross over into an old quarry and turn to the right. On the top of the quarry edge a few yards ahead is a stile. A short scramble brings you to this stile, and across the pasture ahead lies the Tyndale Monument.

The view across the Severn Vale is quite special, so much so that a topograph marks the spot. You can assess the visibility from the landmarks you can see. On a good day, the Sugar Loaf Mountain (33 miles) should be visible. The Severn Bridge is shown as being 12 miles away, whilst nearer to hand is the village of Kingswood (2 miles). From the topograph, the return to Wotton is along a 2½ mile section of the Cotswold Way. Directions are unnecessary, with the route being heavily waymarked. Simply look out for yellow arrows accompanied by white dots, as these appear on trees, stiles and marker posts. The Way passes through Westridge Wood, before crossing open fields to reach the viewpoint on Wotton Hill. Beyond Wotton Hill, the path drops down the hillside to reach the B4060. Turn left, and follow the pavement for ½ mile back to the war memorial and St Mary the Virgin church.

Hillsley
The Fleece

The Fleece, deep in the Southwolds, is a reminder of the great wool days of the Cotswold Hills. The neighbouring Kilcott valley once provided water-power for cloth manufacturing, whilst in 1830 one villager – George Oldland – patented a rotary machine for shearing cloth.

The Fleece is a black-and-white building – white plaster rendering and black paintwork – with a fine Cotswold stone roof. The public bar and the lounge are best described as being very traditional – black wooden beams, hanging tankards, brasses, prints and an open log fire. Two large reproduction prints in the lounge depict scenes from the local cloth industry in bygone days. Perhaps the best tradition maintained by the Fleece is peace and quiet – there is no piped music, neither are there gaming machines or juke boxes, quite simply a friendly atmosphere for pleasant conversation and relaxation.

A good range of bar food is available that covers starters, salads, fish dishes, grills, light snacks and sweets, as well as chef's specials that are available each evening. Knowing precisely what dishes to detail is quite a problem, such is the range of choice. Perhaps snails in garlic butter or home-made pate would go down well as a starter. Main courses could include trout from nearby Alderley, either as part of a salad or grilled with fresh vegetables and potatoes, or the Fleece mixed salad consisting of ham, pate and cheese. The sweets include raspberry meringue, banana split or the most tempting chef's home-made fruit pie. This is a Whitbread house with Whitbread PA on tap, although other good ales such as Flowers, Marston's or Wadworth Bitter could well be available. Whisky buffs will find a good selection of malt whiskies to hand. In fine weather, your refreshments can be enjoyed in the garden to the rear of the Fleece, although the view encompasses little other than the inn itself. Being just off the Cotswold Way amidst fine walking country, the Fleece is well patronised by the walking fraternity. Do heed the notice on the door, however, and leave muddy boots outside the bar.

Telephone: Dursley 843189.

How to get there: Hillsley is a workaday village 3 miles south of Wotton-under-Edge on the unclassified road leading to Hawkesbury. The Fleece Inn has a prominent location in the centre of the village.

Parking: There is a car park at the rear of the Fleece, as well as room for roadside parking in the village itself.

Length of the walk: 4 miles. Map: OS Landranger 172 Bristol and Bath (GR 769896).

The Kilcott valley carries a stream whose power was harnessed by a number of local mills, whilst on the high wolds are the ancient sheep pastures. The woollen industry may be history now, but a fertile imagination could quite easily recreate the scenes of the past. It is this typical Cotswold landscape that this walk explores, the sheltered valleys and the exposed hilltops. An added attraction is the Somerset Monument, high on the Cotswold escarpment, where a climb of 145 steps will reward you with exceptional views of the Southern Cotswolds, the Severn Vale and the distant Welsh Hills.

The Walk

From the Fleece, turn right and walk the short distance to the Portcullis, a one-time hostelry that is now a popular restaurant. Turn right in front of the Portcullis and follow the Kilcott Road out of Hillsley, passing the village school and the Baptist chapel before reaching open countryside. In ½ mile, you will pass an old mill alongside a calm, timeless mill-pond, followed shortly by Lower Kilcott Farm with its adjoining ponds. All the while, your steps will have been paralleled by a tributary stream of the Little Avon river that flows north-westwards to join the Severn near Berkeley. Quarter of a mile on from the farm, you will reach the tiny hamlet of Lower Kilcott. Turn right opposite a group of cottages to follow a bridlepath uphill. This enclosed path is in fact a section of the Cotswold Way, and is clearly signposted.

In just 200 yards, keep left at a fork and continue following the enclosed path uphill until it ends at a gateway. In just a few yards, bear right through a second gateway and follow the left-hand boundary of the field beyond to its far left-hand corner. This open field lies high on the wolds and brings rewarding views northwards of the Cotswold escarpment above Wotton-under-Edge, as well as views of Splatt's Wood in the valley immediately to hand. In the corner of this field you will find two stiles leading into Claypit Wood. The left-hand stile is the footpath, the gateway and stile ahead the bridlepath. Both paths follow a parallel route through this fine deciduous woodland, although the bridlepath is more likely to resemble a quagmire! The paths converge in a little over ¼ mile at the far side of the woodland, which in spring and early summer is awash with wild garlic, bluebells, wood anemones and all those other ever-so-English wild flowers. Leave the woodland and bear half-right, aiming for the large tin barn at the far side of the field ahead. The field-path emerges onto the Hawkesbury to Hillsley road alongside the barn, where a detour of ¼ mile uphill to the left will enable you to visit the Somerset Monument. The vast stone edifice was erected in 1846 in memory of General Robert Edward Henry Somerset, a member of the Beaufort family whose ancestral home was nearby Badminton.

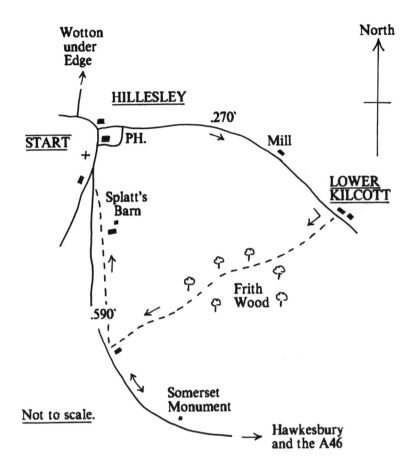

Wotton under Edge

HILLESLEY

270'

START

PH.

Mill

LOWER KILCOTT

Splatt's Barn

North

Frith Wood

590'

Somerset Monument

Not to scale.

Hawkesbury and the A46

Retrace your steps to the barn, and follow the bridlepath directly ahead that follows a parallel course to the Hillsley road. (*NB*. If you do not visit the Somerset Monument, the bridlepath back to Hillsley will be a right-turn when you reach the barn from Claypit Wood.) It heads across the hilltop for ½ mile before passing Splatt's Barn. Beyond this complex of farm buildings, the path descends through an area of woodland before rejoining the Hillsley road a few hundred yards to the south of the village. Follow this quiet road back into the village, passing the Victorian St Giles' church on your left a short distance before you return to the Fleece.

Sherston
The Rattlebone

The Rattlebone is named after one John Rattlebone, a local knight, who fought bravely in 1016 in a battle involving the Danes under King Canute and the forces of Edmund Ironside. Rattlebone was later awarded the manor of Sherston.

The inn dates back to the 17th century, and is whitewashed stone with a traditional Cotswold stone roof. Aside from a games bar and a lounge, there is a fine dining room accommodated in an old outbuilding, as well as an attractive walled garden. The roof space in the dining room is literally festooned with a vast collection of hanging beer bottles, wine bottles and tankards, a most unusual sight. The lounge has a relaxing atmosphere, with its wooden beams and exposed stonework. There are a number of high-backed wooden settles, as well as cushioned window seats, whilst the walls are decorated with an interesting selection of local maps, prints and photographs. Completing the scene is a vast stone fireplace.

A number of tempting dishes are available at the Rattlebone. For starters, quails' eggs or salmon pate form unusual choices. Main courses include fettucini, delice of salmon, rump steak julienne and medallions of lamb, all served with delicious sauces and trimmings, whilst the sweets include brandy snaps and cream, lemon syllabub, fruit pavlova and apple pie. These bar meals are served both at lunchtimes and in the evenings, whilst the normal bar fare – ploughman's, baked potatoes and so on – is available only at lunchtime. The range of beers is equally tempting. Butcombe Bitter, Archers, Wadworth, Beamish Stout and John Smith's Yorkshire Bitter are usually on tap, together with a more unusual guest ale.

Inns like the Rattlebone illustrate just how far pub food has advanced in recent years. The standard of fare is certainly high enough to keep well established restaurants on their toes!

Telephone: Malmesbury 840871.

How to get there: The Rattlebone Inn lies at the northern end of Sherston's High Street, opposite the village church. Sherston lies 6 miles west of Malmesbury on the B4040 Old Sodbury road.

Parking: There is a small car park alongside the Rattlebone for patrons. A better alternative is to park in Sherston's wide High Street, which is literally next door to the inn.

Length of the walk: 6½ miles. Map: OS Landranger 173 Swindon and Devizes (GR 854859).

Sherston lies on the south-eastern fringes of the Cotswolds, amidst a landscape that owes more to its native Wiltshire surroundings than the limestone of the Cotswolds. Whilst this walk passes through countryside that is pleasant, if a little undistinguished, the various attractions along the route make this a worthwhile excursion. Sherston itself, with its wide High Street and ancient church, is worth an hour of anybody's time. There is a lengthy section of the Fosse Way, hereabouts a secluded green lane, that includes an old packhorse bridge across the infant Bristol Avon. Finally, there is the picturesque village of Easton Grey, which is pure Cotswold in character and feel. This stone village is centred upon a five-arched bridge that spans the Avon, although its main features of interest – Easton Grey House and the church – lie on the northern edge of the settlement. The house is known as a 'boutique-in-a-garden', being the family home of a fashion designer whose garments can be purchased locally. An undulating excursion that has none of the climbs or gradients found further north in the Cotswold hills.

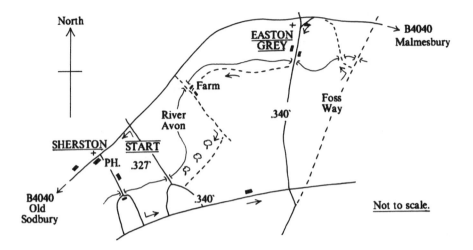

The Walk

The walk begins by taking a right-turn just past the Rattlebone Inn into Noble Street. Follow the pavement on down to Tanners Hill and across the Sherston branch of the river Avon. There is also a Tetbury branch, but because of local disagreement over the actual source of the Avon, both are allowed to stand on the OS sheets! Just beyond the river, the road forks. Bear left up Bustlers Hill to a second road junction in less than ½ mile. Turn left, and follow the lane signposted to Foxley. This lane is followed for the next 1½ miles until it is crossed by a byway that is actually the Fosse Way; 1 mile to New Barn, 700 yards further to a crossroads and then just 100 yards to the Fosse Way. Turn left and follow the Fosse Way, the ancient Roman road that ran from Lincoln to Exeter, for just over ½ mile, to a point where it ceases to be an enclosed green lane and enters an open field. The Fosse Way descends to an ancient stone bridge across the Avon – well worth making the appropriate detour – whilst our path is the well-used field track that bears to the left towards the far corner of the field and a gateway.

In the next field, follow the right-hand field boundary, the Avon in the valley to the right, before passing through a pair of gates to reach an old mill complex and a stone bridge across the Avon. This splendidly isolated spot is an ideal place in which to cool tired feet and enjoy a rest break. Cross the Avon and follow the path ahead uphill through a wooded and overgrown hillside to reach arable farmland. Literally follow the left-hand field boundaries of the next two fields until you reach a gateway that leads onto the B4040 Sherston to

Malmesbury road. Turn left and, in 400 yards, take the left-turn at a crossroads to follow a quiet lane down into Easton Grey village. The church is on your right before the lane drops into the village. Cottages, farms and barns are collected together on a bankside above the Avon.

Cross the river by means of the fine old stone bridge and, in just 20 yards, turn right through a handgate and climb the rise ahead into an open field. Cross this large open pasture to its far right-hand corner, where a pair of gates and stiles leads into the adjoining field. Here it is the same procedure again – make for the dip in the far right-hand corner, where a stile brings you into a third field, up above the Avon. Follow the right-hand field boundary in this field around to Park Farm, where the path passes between a house and a barn into the farmyard itself before emerging onto a stony farm road. Turn left, follow this farm track uphill for 400 yards, before passing through some iron gates into Pinkney Park. Continue along this path for ½ mile until it joins a quiet country lane. Turn right and, in 200 yards, right at a junction. Cross the Avon and follow the road uphill back into Sherston. Shortly, you will join the B4040 where you turn left to return to the centre of the village.

NB. This walk contains a high proportion of road walking, albeit along quiet lanes and byways. If you could manage a longer excursion of some 9 miles, it is possible to reach the Fosse Way due south of Sherston by way of an ancient bridlepath – Commonwood Lane. This would then enable you to walk a 3 mile section of the Fosse Way from the main South Wales railway to the packhorse bridge across the Avon. I refer interested readers to OS Pathfinder sheet 1152!

Old Sodbury
The Dog Inn

The Dog fronts onto the busy A432 road, and lacks the picturesque location of many other Cotswold inns. However, do not let the roar of traffic put you off for here is a pub that offers one of the finest selections of food in the area.

Externally, the Dog is pink-stucco with a tiled roof, little original stonework being exposed. The traditional building materials are more clearly displayed on the interior, where a wealth of stonework has been exposed and a plethora of wooden beams restored to pristine condition. There is one long bar, with ample tables and seating, with two traditional open fireplaces adding to the warm atmosphere. Families are adequately catered for with a separate family room and a large beer garden that comes complete with children's rides.

An excellent range of beers, wines and spirits is available at the bar, including the ever-popular Wadworth 6X, as well as an interesting Broad Oak cider. It is food, however, in which the Dog excels. If I say that the menu displays over 100 main choices, then you will perhaps forgive me for not going into too much detail. Naturally, there are sandwiches, ploughman's, salads and grills, but beyond this your choice could range over crab americaine, snails soaked in champagne and served with garlic butter, scallops Devon style and Greek village salad. There are over a dozen vegetarian selections, mussels and squid, fresh fish dishes and 'puppy-food', the Dog's ingenious name for its children's menu. This huge range of choice extends to the sweets, where alongside the traditional spotted dick with custard, we find chocolate au cointreau and pear belle helene. The menu stresses that all meals and sauces are freshly prepared and cooked to order. This does, inevitably, mean some degree of patience may be required, but this is but a small price to pay for what are first-rate meals, served in more than ample portions. Perhaps a meal at the Dog serves as a timely reminder as to how bland much of the fast-food available elsewhere has become.

Telephone: Chipping Sodbury 312006.

How to get there: The Dog Inn lies on the A432 Chipping Sodbury to Old Sodbury road, a mile before its junction with the A46.

Parking: There is a car park alongside the Dog Inn, whilst the two minor roads that join the A432 alongside the inn – Chapel Lane and Cotswold Lane – both offer ample roadside parking.

Length of the walk: 3 miles. Map: OS Landranger 172 Bristol and Bath (GR 754815).

Old Sodbury lies on the Cotswold Way, on the fringes of the Southwolds. The 800 year old church, dedicated to St John the Baptist, sits proudly on the Cotswold escarpment overlooking the Severn plain, whilst a mile or two to the north at Little Sodbury is St Adeline's church, standing on the former village green. The fine medieval manor at Little Sodbury was where William Tyndale was employed as tutor between 1522 and 1523. The high hilltops above Old and Little Sodbury are the site of a vast Iron Age hillfort. Enclosing a site of some eleven acres, this rectangular multivallate fort later played host to both Roman and Saxon armies. This short ramble explores the countryside at the foot of the scarp between Old and Little Sodbury, before returning by way of the hilltops and the hillfort. The climb from Little Sodbury to Sodbury Fort is little more than 200 ft in about ½ mile, nothing too strenuous and well within the confines of most walkers.

The Walk

Cross the road opposite the Dog and follow the lane opposite – Cotswold Lane – for just ¼ mile until you reach St John the Baptist church on the left-hand side. Inside the 800 year old church are a pair of effigies, one unusually carved out of wood and dedicated to Philip

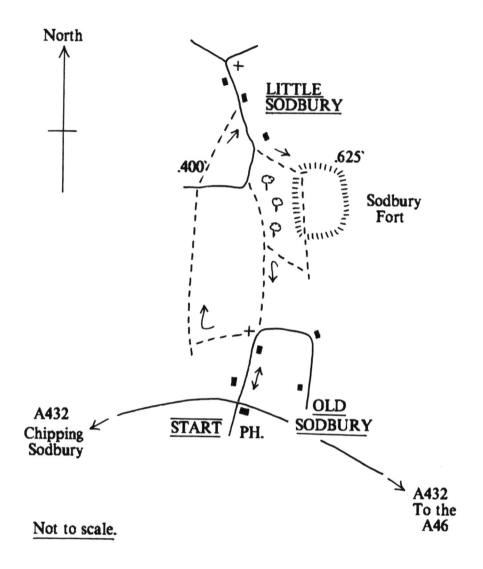

North

LITTLE
SODBURY

.400'

.625'

Sodbury
Fort

A432
Chipping
Sodbury

START / PH.

OLD
SODBURY

A432
To the
A46

Not to scale.

le Gros. My favourite spot around the church, however, is the seat at
the western end of the churchyard which commands fine views of the
Severn Vale. Pass through the kissing-gate alongside this seat, and
follow the path downhill to the hedgerow at the foot of the hill. Turn
right, and follow this hedgerow along the bottom of the field, your
steps paralleled by a series of telegraph wires. At the far side of this

field, pass to the right of a pond before crossing a stile in the hedgerow ahead. Follow the right-hand field boundaries through the next four fields, the telegraph lines your constant companions, until you reach Portway Lane, a quiet byway that leads from Little Sodbury to Chipping Sodbury. Cross the road and the stile opposite into an open field, whose bumps and humps are described on the OS sheet as 'Pillow Mounds'. Aim for the far right-hand corner of this field, where a stile brings you onto a lane leading into Little Sodbury. A brief detour to your left will enable you to visit St Adeline's church, built as recently as 1859 on what was formerly the village green. It replaced a church of the same dedication that originally stood on the hill above the manor. The rest of the village consists essentially of scattered farmhouses and cottages.

Retrace your steps along the lane, which climbs for ½ mile out of the village. Turn left at the top of the hill onto a driveway that leads to the private manor, and almost immediately turn right onto a track that heads uphill to Sodbury Fort. Continue straight uphill to the ramparts, ignoring a waymarked left-turn as you ascend the hillside. Although the fort dates from the Iron Age, it is a site of multi-occupancy. In 1471, for example, Edward IV rested here before moving on to destroy the army of Margaret of Anjou at the Battle of Tewkesbury. Cross to the far right-hand side of the fort, that is the southern ramparts, beyond which you will find a stile in the wall beneath an imposing sycamore tree. Turn right immediately beyond the stile to follow what is the Cotswold Way downhill through Little Sodbury Wood. At the foot of the hill, as you emerge from the trees, turn left to follow the waymarked Cotswold Way across a stile and into a hillside field. Continue along the right-hand field boundary for almost ½ mile to the far right-hand corner of the field, where a stile leads onto an enclosed path that very soon emerges onto Cotswold Lane alongside St John's church. Retrace your steps back along the lane to the Dog Inn.

Castle Combe
The White Hart

The White Hart Inn stands at the northern end of Castle Combe's main street, directly opposite the ancient market cross. The White Hart is a charming old inn, with its whitewashed walls and stone-tiled roof. Internally, there is one main bar together with a family room, whilst to the rear of the inn is an attractive beer garden with a number of picnic tables. The main bar, with its flagstone flooring and wooden beams, conveys a very rural feel. This effect is enhanced by a fine open fireplace and low ceilings. The furnishings consist of wooden tables, high-backed wooden settles and cushioned window seats, whilst around the walls are displayed prints, photographs and various items of rural memorabilia. These include a rather fine horse harness and several old cider pots. The adjoining family room is more simply furnished, with a good number of tables and chairs offering ample accommodation for younger visitors.

The White Hart offers a good selection of snacks and bar meals, which are colourfully listed on blackboards alongside the bar. The normal bar fayre of salads, sandwiches, steaks and ploughman's is naturally available, together with a number of less traditional offerings. These might typically include king prawns in garlic butter, Cumberland sausages filled with cheese and rolled in bacon, chicken tikka on a bed of rice, deep fried Brie and cranberry sauce and red hot chilli con carne. As befits an inn with a family room, children are not forgotten. Their menu runs to all of the old favourites – burgers, sausages, eggs, ham and chips – as well as smaller portions of some of the main menu dishes. The sweets available include lemon meringue pie, chocolate fudge cake, apple pie and a selection of ice creams. The White Hart also offers a good selection of beers and ales. These include offerings from such illustrious brewers as Ushers, Ruddles, Wadworth and Tetley.

I was impressed with the White Hart. Castle Combe has become very popular with tourists over the years, and I had expected this to have a somewhat detrimental impact on the village pub. Fortunately, this is not the case. It is a hostelry where locals have not had changes inflicted upon their pub by the demands of visitors. The food prices are still very reasonable, and the decor represents just what one would expect of the traditional English village public house.

Telephone: Castle Combe 782295.

How to get there: Castle Combe lies just to the south of the B4039 Acton Turville to Chippenham road. As you enter the village from Upper Castle Combe, the White Hart lies on the left-hand side opposite the market cross.

Parking: There is no car park at the White Hart, and on the road outside the inn there are spaces for no more than a dozen cars to park. As you enter the village from Upper Castle Combe, however, there is roadside parking for a number of cars about 200 yards from the White Hart.

Length of the walk: 3½ miles. Map: OS Landranger 173 Swindon and Devizes (GR 843773).

Castle Combe is undoubtedly one of Britain's most attractive villages. Its golden cottages nestle at the foot of a charming valley, made even more beautiful by the sparkling waters of the By Brook. With all of the classic Cotswold architecture, the parish church and the market cross, the village has become justifiably popular with visitors to the area. This walk explores not only the village, but also some of the fine natural landscape in the surrounding area. This includes both a dry river valley, fine deciduous woodland, traditional meadows and the banks of the By Brook, a noted trout stream. Much of this landscape is a nature reserve managed by the Wiltshire Trust for Nature Conservation, and is therefore of quite exceptional quality. A fine ramble that proves that the Southwolds have much to offer for the rambler who believes that the wolds end at Cirencester!

The Walk

From the White Hart, head out of Castle Combe along the road that leads back to the B4039. In 300 yards, opposite a cottage named Hillhouse, turn right onto a bridlepath that is signposted to Upper Castle Combe. This stony track climbs the hillside for about 400 yards before joining a lane, where you turn left to walk into Upper Castle Combe itself. In the centre of the village, at the road junction, continue straight ahead along the main Chippenham road for just 100 yards, before turning left onto an unclassified road that runs alongside the rear of a chapel. Follow this quiet lane for ½ mile to a T-junction, where you turn right onto a signposted byway. This is a delightful green lane, that follows a shady course between the fields down to the B4039.

Follow the verge alongside this occasionally busy road for just 200 yards, passing one entrance to the Castle Combe race track, until you come to three gateways in quick succession on the right-hand side. Pass through the final one of these – a small handgate – which is the start of a bridlepath that we will follow for the next mile through to Long Dean. The path initially passes to the left of Kent's Bottom Farm, before passing through a field-gate on the left-hand side just 30 yards on from the farmhouse. Beyond this gate, the clearly defined bridlepath continues alongside an open field, the embankments of the race track to the right. At the next gate, the path enters a nature reserve managed by the Wiltshire Trust for Nature Conservation. There is woodland on both sides of the path at first, before it enters an open field. Head across this open space, passing to the right of an enclosed drain cover, and pass through a gate that takes the path into Hammerdown Wood. An all too short section of path passes through this fine area of deciduous woodland before it emerges into an open field. Bear to the right and follow the field-path along the side of the valley ahead. This is a really attractive dry river valley, where traditional patterns of land management have preserved an abundance of flora and fauna. The wild flowers in the area – clover, trefoil, scabious, ragged robin and thistles – attract a rich variety of butterflies.

This path along the steep-sided valley eventually bears to the left to join the lane leading from Castle Combe to Giddeahall. Turn left at the road and, almost immediately, right onto a cul-de-sac lane that leads down to the marvellously secluded hamlet of Long Dean. Just as you enter this settlement, take the first turning on the right-hand side which becomes a footpath leading back to Castle Combe. Beyond

110

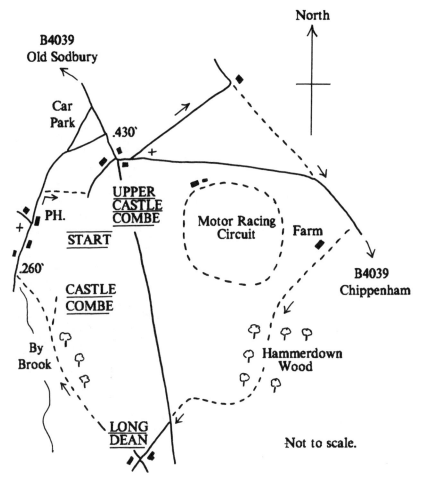

North

B4039
Old Sodbury

Car
Park

.430'

UPPER
CASTLE
COMBE

PH.

START

.260'

CASTLE
COMBE

By
Brook

Motor Racing
Circuit

Farm

B4039
Chippenham

Hammerdown
Wood

LONG
DEAN

Not to scale.

Rose Cottage, the path climbs up the hillside to follow a woodland path high on the hillside above the By Brook. Again, this land is managed by the WTNC whose traditional methods of management mean a high quality landscape. The path passes out of the woodland into an open field, where the right of way bears to the left downhill towards the By Brook. In no time at all, a stone footbridge crosses the brook to bring you out onto the Castle Combe road. Turn right, and follow the road alongside By Brook back into the village, keeping a sharp eye out for the numerous trout in its clear waters. Incidentally, see if you can spot a clever sign that hangs above a low doorway on North Cottage, just on your left as you enter Castle Combe. It reads quite simply 'Duck or Grouse'!

111

Ford
The White Hart

This walk begins by following a 1 mile section of bridlepath described on the OS Pathfinder sheet as 'The Old Coach Road'. This provides a clue as to the origins of the White Hart, where we find a stone fireplace inscribed with the date 1553. Certainly, the coaching timetables record services operating from London to Bristol that stopped at the inn at Ford.

Today, the White Hart still stands close to the main A420 Bristol road, now thankfully a much quieter route than in the 1960s due to the opening of the M4 motorway. The inn is a delightful stone building, with a pleasant location alongside the sparkling waters of the By Brook. The public bar is furnished with a number of well polished wooden tables and chairs, with black beams and white ceiling panels creating a relaxed and welcoming atmosphere. Prints, photographs and advertising mirrors adorn the walls, including one that extols the virtues of the now sadly defunct Georges beer, a one-time Bristol brew. Adjoining the public bar is the lounge, where families are welcome to enjoy the White Hart's hospitality. On hot days, visitors to the inn have the option of enjoying their refreshment either on the small number of picnic tables in front of the inn, or on a grassed area that overlooks the By Brook.

The White Hart offers a regular bar menu that contains all of the traditional favourites – ploughman's, sandwiches, salads, gammon, steak, scampi, chicken, steak and kidney pie – as well as a number of daily specials that are chalked up above the bar. On a recent visit, these included vegetable crumble, liver and onions, lamb goulash, lasagne and beef casserole. The dishes were reasonably priced, of ample proportions and well presented. The excellent selection of beers is, perhaps, the White Hart's most well known feature. It is not unusual to find up to a dozen real ales available. These would normally include Tanglefoot, Badger Best, Fullers ESB, Greene King Abbot and Smiles Exhibition. There is also a guest beer available, Uley Old Spot being the selection when I last visited the White Hart.

CAMRA's 'Wiltshire Pub Guide' describes the White Hart as being a 'superb old inn full of atmosphere'. Whether your forte is real ale, good pub food, traditional pub architecture or rustic charm, I am certain that you would echo CAMRA's sentiments.

Telephone: Castle Combe 782213.

How to get there: Ford lies on the A420 road midway between Chippenham and Marshfield. The White Hart lies just off the main road, along the unclassified road leading to Colerne.

Parking: There is parking at the White Hart for patrons. Alternatively, a lay-by on the A420 opposite Ford church provides parking for a small number of vehicles.

Length of the walk: 4 miles. Map: OS Landranger 173 Swindon and Devizes (GR 842747).

This ramble explores the countryside around three Southwolds villages – Ford, North Wraxall and Slaughterford. Whilst none of these villages lie on the main tourist routes, each is an excellent example of a typical Cotswold settlement, with its church, stone cottages and surrounding farms. Whilst the local residents are now more likely to be retired folk or Bath and Bristol businessmen, each village still maintains its traditional rural charm. The surrounding countryside will perhaps hold greatest appeal. Here we find valleys and hillsides, traditional woodland and sparkling streams, the very ingredients that make the Cotswolds such a paradise for walkers. The woodland paths can be damp and muddy, and the hillside slopes are steep in places, but all-in-all this is a ramble that should present no difficulties for an active family group.

The Walk

From the White Hart, walk the few yards to the nearby A420 and turn left. On the opposite side of the road lies the village church, beyond which the Old Coach Road leaves the modern highway. Follow this Old Coach Road westwards for over a mile to the neighbouring village of North Wraxhall. For the first 200 yards as it climbs out of Ford, it is a quiet tarmac lane giving access to a number of cottages. Beyond the last dwelling – Quarry Barn – it continues as an unmetalled bridleway, giving occasional views to the south across the nearby valley to New Wood.

The bridlepath eventually joins the lane leading into North Wraxall alongside a bungalow. Turn right at this lane, and head towards the village. In a short distance, you will pass Southwood Cottage on the right-hand side which is followed almost immediately by the 'North Wraxall' sign on the left-hand verge. Just before this sign, turn left onto an unmarked footpath that climbs the roadside bank and heads down to the A420. A detour will be necessary if you wish to visit the village itself. The main point of interest in the village will prove to be St James' church, which, although mainly 13th century in origin, does contain an earlier south doorway and arch. Within the church lies the Methuen Chapel and a ceiling decorated with 35 heraldic shields arranged in a family tree.

Cross the A420 and follow the track opposite for 100 yards to a bungalow. Follow the right-hand path alongside this dwelling, which drops steeply down into an area of woodland before an ancient stone bridge crosses the stream at the foot of the hill. The stream is the Doncombe Brook, a tributary of the By Brook, whilst the OS Pathfinder map appropriately labels the crossing as 'Stoney Bridge'. The path bears to the right on the far side of the water before forking. Take the left-hand fork which climbs the hillside up through the trees. At the first crossing, turn left and continue following the main path through the woodland. In about 250 yards, there is another fork where we bear right to enter an open field. Follow the left-hand side of this field alongside the woodland to a gateway and the Ford to Colerne road. Cross this lane, and follow the byway opposite signposted to Euridge. The protected verges that line this lane are awash with wild flowers in the spring and summer months, whilst the drystone walls are a delight to behold.

This hilltop lane, with extensive views, is followed for 200 yards until you reach a gateway on the left-hand side and a stony track that leads down to Colerne Down Farmhouse. Follow this path downhill, ignoring any paths and tracks that join or leave the main track, until you reach a group of cottages on the left-hand side. All the while the

114

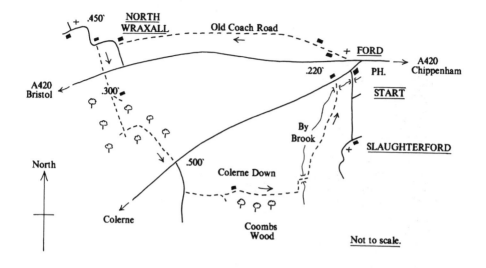

views across the By Brook valley towards Ford and Slaughterford are quite superb. A short distance beyond these cottages, the path forks. Bear to the right and continue along the path to a field gate. Beyond this gate, continue directly ahead following an obvious path alongside Coombs Wood. At the far side of the field, cross a stile into the next field and keep straight on until you reach the south bank of By Brook. This is a quite delightful stream, whose crystal clear waters are home to any number of trout. Fishing rights are naturally jealously guarded!

Turn left and follow the river bank for 200 yards to a metal bridge that crosses the brook alongside a weir. (Incidentally, should you wish to visit Slaughterford then another detour is necessary. This involves turning right when you reach the river and crossing a network of sluices and footbridges into the village.) Once across the metal bridge, turn left and follow the well-used path across the next four fields back into Ford. All the while, your steps are paralleled by the By Brook which meanders its way across the meadowland on your left. You will enter the fourth field by crossing another metal bridge over the brook alongside a weir. Beyond this bridge, follow the By Brook for a few yards before bearing left to follow a feeder stream out onto the Ford to Colerne road. At the road, turn right and in less than ¼ mile you will be back at the White Hart.

Lansdown Hill
The Blathwayt Arms

The Blathwayt Arms was known originally as 'The Star'. The rather more impressive 'modern' name is derived from William Blathwayte, one-time Clerk to the Privy Council for the reigns of Charles II, James II, William and Mary, and Queen Anne. He married into the Wynter family of nearby Dyrham in 1686, and by 1690 had acquired much of the high ground north of Bath known as Lansdown.

The Blathwayt Arms has undergone a great deal of renovation in recent years, and has perhaps lost some of its earlier character and feel. The lounge, bar and dining area are light and airy, and furnished with a good number of reproduction tables and chairs. The bar areas are carpeted, whilst the original stone walls have been lost beneath plaster and wallpaper. Wooden beams and clever use of partitioning, however, mean that the Blathwayt Arms has still managed to retain a little of its warmth and atmosphere. To the rear of the inn is an excellent family garden, with as many as 50 picnic tables for patrons to use. Many of these nestle beneath mature tree cover which provides welcome shade from the summer sun, whilst the nearby play-area keeps energetic youngsters amused.

The bar menu at this Whitebread hostelry offers a good selection of dishes. These include appetizers, main courses, vegetarian dishes, specialities, salads, sandwiches, ploughman's and sweets. For an appetizer, crispy fried potato skins is an unusual option, whilst the main courses include honey-glazed chicken, Cumberland sausage and the Landlord's grill. This grill contains rump steak, lamb cutlet, sausage, kidney, gammon, tomato and mushroom. The specialities include sirloin au poivre, pork escalope in cider sauce, rainbow trout and chicken kiev. Children are not forgotten, with a menu that includes old favourites like sausages, burgers and fish fingers. A number of good beers are available at the Blathwayt Arms. These include brews from Flowers, Boddingtons and Wadworth, as well as the increasingly popular Murphy's Stout.

Telephone: Bath 421995.

How to get there: Lansdown Hill lies on the unclassified road that leads northwards from Bath to the A420 at Wick. The Blathwayt Arms lies alongside this road, 3 miles north of Bath's city centre, adjoining the local racecourse.

Parking: There is a large car park alongside the Blathwayt Arms.

Length of the walk: 6 miles. Map: OS Landranger 172 Bristol and Bath (GR 725686).

To the north of Bath, the southern flanks of the Cotswold Hills come tumbling down towards the Avon. This impressive hill country provides some of the finest walking in the area. As well as delightful hamlets and villages, the natural landscape is quite outstanding. Deep valleys, high hilltops and expansive views abound, rivalling anything that can be found in the northern wolds. This ramble explores the area around Lansdown Hill, just 3 miles north of Bath. Spectacular viewpoints bring views across both Bath and Bristol, whilst in the depths of the valleys there is an unusual remoteness for a walk that runs so close to a major city. The price to be paid for the heights, however, is a substantial hill climb – the final mile of the walk sees 450 ft of climbing!

The Walk

Just to the south of the Blathwayt Arms, a single-bar metal stile leads onto Bath racecourse. At the spectator's rail ahead, turn right and walk towards the stands, ¼ mile distant. Where you meet an enclosure, just before the stand, bear left and head directly across the track to the right-hand edge of the trees that line the far side of the course. This involves ducking beneath a number of rails and fences that mark out the racecourse itself. (Incidentally, should there be a race-meeting taking place, you would have to follow the perimeter fence all the way

117

round the racecourse.) Follow the edge of the hilltop around to the right, continuing beyond a stile in the corner of the field onto a second stile which brings a quite spectacular view. This is Prospect Stile, one of just a handful of stiles actually named on the OS sheets. The prospect is certainly impressive – one of the best views in the Bath and Bristol area. Rather than actually crossing this stile, continue along the field boundary to its right, along the edge of the hilltop, until you reach a gate and stile in the field boundary ahead. This takes you out of the racecourse enclosure and out into open countryside.

Since Prospect Stile, our steps have followed the Cotswold Way, a path that we continue along for the next 3 miles. The Cotswold Way is well signposted with coloured arrows and accompanying dots, so you can proceed for a time without necessarily following the directions which follow.

Continue along the field boundary ahead to the corner of the field, and bear right for just 100 yards. Turn left into the adjoining field at a marker post, and cross the open field ahead. This hilltop is the site of an ancient hillfort, a refuge when settlements lower down the hillside were under attack. At the far side of this field, head downhill for 50 yards to a junction of paths. Turn right, following the familiar Cotswold Way waymark, and head across a narrow enclosure for 200 yards to a stile at the far side of the field. Continue along the hilltop track ahead, a path which very soon borders Brockham Wood and the adjoining Lansdown Golf Course. Shortly, when you reach a stone barn on the right, fork right and continue along the path to a cross-track. Turn left and follow the Cotswold Way for just ½ mile to the triangulation pillar on Hanging Hill. This 771 ft hilltop brings fine views across the eastern outskirts of Bristol. Turn right at the trig point, to follow the waymarked Cotswold Way around the Observer Corps buidings, past Beach Wood and out onto the Lansdown road.

Cross this road, and continue along the Cotswold Way for just a few yards to the Grenville Monument. The full story of this spot where Sir Bevill Grenville was killed during the Civil War is told on a plaque. The Way passes to the right of the monument before winding through some woodland and up into an arable field. Follow the left-hand edge of this field to a stile on the far side, beyond which you will join a cross-track. Turn left and follow this rough track downhill for 1 mile to a group of farm buildings. Some way down this enclosed path, the Cotswold Way crosses a stile on the left to continue on its course towards Chipping Campden, whilst our path brings magnificent views of the valley below carrying the diminutive Lam Brook. On the far side of the valley, the heavy traffic crawling up the A46 towards the M4 motorway is clearly visible.

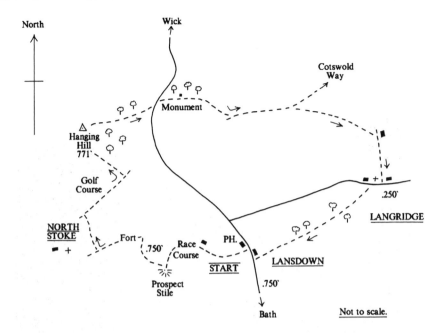

North

Wick

Cotswold Way

Monument

Hanging Hill 771'

Golf Course

.250'

LANGRIDGE

NORTH STOKE

Fort

.750'

Race Course

PH.

LANSDOWN

START

Prospect Stile

.750'

Bath

Not to scale.

At the farm buildings, turn right and follow the farm lane downhill for ¼ mile to a T-junction. Turn right and follow the lane through the hamlet of Langridge, passing a traditional stone farm and the Norman church of St Mary Magdalen. As you climb through the village, look out for a bungalow on the right-hand side called Court Mead. Opposite this bungalow, pass through the gateway on the left and cross two fields to reach a dip in the bottom of the second field. The small stream in this dip has its source in the many springs that bubble from the surrounding hillsides.

Cross the stream and bear right uphill, following the hedgerow on the right. At the top of the field, following a climb of 150 ft, pass through a gate in a clump of trees into the next field. Head across this field, a climb of some 200 ft this time, to a stile in the wall on the far side. This involves bearing slightly to the left as you cross the field, keeping your eye open for an arrowed marker post pointing the final few yards up to the stile. Incidentally, the views all of the way up from Langridge are exceptional. On the many occasions you will inevitably pause for breath, don't forget to look back across the quite superb Cotswold landscape. Beyond the stile, continue ahead to a stony farm track. Turn right, and in just a few minutes you will be back on the Bath to Wick road. A few yards along on the left-hand side lies the Blathwayt Arms, welcome relief after the final climb up from Langridge!

119

Avoncliff
The Cross Guns

Avoncliff is a remote hamlet, deep in the Avon valley between Bath and Bradford-on-Avon. A pair of flock mills on the river gave rise to the settlement, but it was the coming of the canal in the late 18th century that most influenced life in the valley. The Cross Guns dates back to the 17th century, and was therefore frequented by the local weavers long before it became a bargees watering hole. The inn enjoys a most attractive location, sandwiched between the Kennet and Avon Canal and the river Avon. The terraced gardens at the front of the Cross Guns provide excellent views of both the river and the magnificent aqueduct.

The Cross Guns is a marvellously old fashioned pub, with a vast stone fireplace, stone walls, low beams and solid oak tables. The increasing popularity of the inn with walkers, cyclists and canal-users does mean that the small bar area can become very crowded. However, there are a large number of picnic tables on the terraces overlooking the Avon, where food and drink can be enjoyed overlooking the river.

The Cross Guns is developing quite a reputation for the quality of its food. Naturally, the standard pub fare of sandwiches and ploughman's is on offer, but beyond this are a number of most appetising dishes. These could include home-made steak and kidney pie, perhaps preceded by some home-made pate, a variety of steak dishes and a number of fish options. These typically include lemon sole, trout and crab. The Cross Guns is a freehouse, and offers as a consequence an interesting range of beers and ales. These include Tanglefoot, Ruddles BB and County, Smiles BB and Ushers BB.

With its superb location, its traditional interior, the good selection of beers and the fascinating canal architecture, the Cross Guns is a truly excellent pub to visit. It justifiably earns an entry in most good pub guides.

Telephone: Bradford-on-Avon 862335.

How to get there: Avoncliff can be reached either from Bradford-on-Avon, where an unclassified road ends at the northern end of the aqueduct, or from Upper Westwood, where a steep hill descends to the southern end of the aqueduct. The Cross Guns Inn lies at the southern end of the aqueduct.

Parking: There is a public car park at the southern end of the aqueduct, whilst limited roadside parking is available at the northern end of the aqueduct. The limited number of parking spaces in the area do fill up rapidly at weekends, so an early arrival is advised. The inn does not have its own car park.

Length of the walk: 5 miles. Maps: OS Landranger 172 Bristol and Bath and 173 Swindon and Devizes are both needed for this walk (GR 805600).

The Avon valley south of Bath has recently been incorporated into the Cotswold Area of Outstanding Natural Beauty (AONB). With its hillsides, woodland and attractive stone villages, the area has always had the feel of the wolds if not the official designation. As well as an exploration of the valley and its surrounding environs, this walk includes a fine section of the recently restored Kennet and Avon Canal. At Avoncliff and Dundas, two of the finest aqueducts in the south of England were constructed to carry the Kennet and Avon across the river Avon. Both of these constructions are included in this walk, which also visits the hilltop villages of Conkwell and Winsley. A fine ramble that lies geologically at the point where the Cotswold limestone is replaced by the chalk hills of Wessex.

The Walk

Follow the lane outside the Cross Guns that goes underneath Avoncliff Aqueduct. At the far side of this 18th century construction, turn sharp left to secure the canal towpath. Follow the towpath across the aqueduct and along through the Avon valley for just over 2 miles to Dundas with its aqueduct and wharf. The wharf marks the junction with the Somerset Coal Canal, an important feeder route into the Kennet and Avon, whose first ¼ mile has been restored to provide moorings for pleasure craft.

To continue on to Conkwell involves a complete circuit of the wharf and the aqueduct. Follow the towpath around Dundas Wharf, passing the small warehouse and its neighbouring crane, and cross the footbridge beyond to reach the far side of the canal. Turn right, and

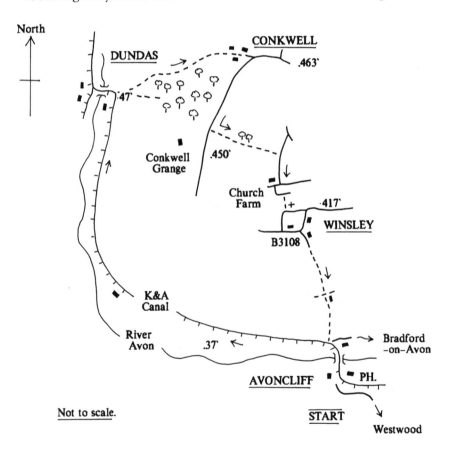

North

CONKWELL

DUNDAS

.463'

.47'

Conkwell
Grange

.450'

Church
Farm

·417'

WINSLEY

B3108

K&A
Canal

River
Avon

.37'

Bradford
-on-Avon

AVONCLIFF

PH.

Not to scale.

START

Westwood

follow the towpath back across the aqueduct, only this time on the opposite bank. The path ends at a stile, which is crossed into Conkwell Woods. Rather than heading straight uphill on what is the bed of an old mineral tramway, look for a stile on the left-hand side. Cross this stile into an open field, head half-right and climb to a stile in the far corner of the field. Fine views extend northwards through the Avon valley, the most recent addition to the Cotswolds AONB. Beyond the stile, follow the path as it borders the edge of the woodland up the hillside into Conkwell.

Conkwell is an interesting settlement, a hamlet that once housed local quarry workers. The first cottage on the right-hand side is named 'Spring Cottage'. Bear right immediately past this cottage, onto a waymarked path. Follow this path through deciduous woodland for about ½ mile, before joining a quiet country lane. Avoid any right turns, especially the one that heads directly downhill back to Dundas! Turn right on reaching the lane, which is followed for ½ mile through open countryside. On a clear day, the Marlborough Downs are visible away to the east, a sure sign that this is the border between the Cotswold limestone and the chalk hills of Wessex. At a bend in the road, near to Conkwell Grange, a stile on the left beneath a tree takes you into an open field. Unfortunately, there is no waymark at this point. Cross this field, aiming for the right of a clump of trees ahead, and follow the right-hand boundary of the next field out onto a country lane. Turn right and head towards Church Farm and Winsley.

Church Farm lies alongside the Winsley bypass. On reaching this road, turn right and, almost immediately, left into Late Broads. This brings you into a new housing development. Take the first turning on the left – Millbourne Close – before turning right onto a footpath that leads up to Winsley church. Turn left in front of the church and continue for the few yards to the B3108 Bradford-on-Avon road. Turn right at this point and walk past the Seven Stars pub. Where the B3108 bears right on its way to Bath, carry straight ahead along a lane that leads to the village hall and the bowling club. Continue along this lane until it ends at a stile just alongside the cricket club.

Follow the enclosed path down the hillside beyond the cricket ground, avoiding the right fork. A quite superb view opens up that extends beyond the Avon valley and Bradford-on-Avon to the distant Wiltshire Downs. The Westbury white horse is but one landmark. The path ends at a kissing-gate where it joins an unmetalled lane. Cross this lane, and follow the path diagonally across the field ahead that leads downhill to Avoncliff. At the bottom of the field, a kissing-gate brings you to Avoncliff Aqueduct. Cross the aqueduct to return to the Cross Guns.

Freshford
The Inn

The Inn at Freshford overlooks the Somerset Frome, a sparkling tributary of the Bristol Avon. It is a picturesque three-storey stone building, attractively decorated with window boxes, hanging baskets and tubs of flowers. The Inn dates from Tudor times.

Internally, the bar area has been comfortably modernised without losing its traditional character. At either end of the lounge are vast stone fireplaces, with a roaring log fire guaranteed in the winter months. Brasses and brassware, china displays, and various rural memorabilia – scythes, yoke and cartwheels – lend The Inn a truly rural feel. This is enhanced by the exposed beams and stonework, including a stone serving counter. The Inn is carpeted throughout, and is furnished with wooden tables and chairs, and cushioned window seats. To the rear of The Inn is a pleasant garden, amply furnished with picnic tables, an ideal resting place after a walk in the hot summer sun.

This is an Ushers house, the local Trowbridge-based brewers. In addition to Ushers brews, however, both Ruddles and Websters Bitters are available at The Inn. To accompany your drink, there is a vast range of food that covers all the normal categories – salads, baked potatoes, ploughman's, sandwiches, vegetarian dishes, fish dishes, grills, children's dishes and specials. A few examples might whet your appetite. Specials might include swordfish, halibut steak hongroise or king prawns, whilst beef wellington, medallions of pork, steak and mushroom pie or chicken kiev regularly adorn the day's menu. Vegetarians might care to choose a nut roast, vegetable lasagne or vegetable curry. All these dishes are served with their own specially prepared sauces. The children's menu includes those old favourites – sausages, fish fingers or burgers – all served quite rightly with chips! The sweet menu is almost as extensive as the main menu. Orange and lemon sorbets, banana split, chocolate truffle torte, profiteroles and death by chocolate will all reinstate those calories worn off during a brisk country stroll. With its excellent choice of dishes, its ample helpings and its attractive location, The Inn at Freshford has earned a deserved reputation in the Bath area.

Telephone: Bath 722250.

How to get there: Freshford lies just off the A36 Bath to Warminster road, 1 mile south of Limpley Stoke. Follow the lane through the village in the direction of Sharpstone and Westwood. The Inn lies on the extreme southern edge of the village, overlooking the Somerset Frome.

Parking: There is a car park for patrons to the rear of The Inn. Roadside parking in the vicinity of The Inn is difficult. A better option for non-patrons is to use the car park at Freshford station, just minutes from The Inn.

Length of the walk: 4 miles. Map: OS Landranger 172 Bristol and Bath (GR 791600).

Freshford lies on the extreme southern boundary of the Cotswolds, a few miles outside Bath, in an area that has only recently been included in the official AONB. The village is clearly Cotswold in character, however, with its golden cottages and houses, its historic associations with the woollen trade, and its location amidst rolling hills and river valleys.

This walk, on the southern fringes of the Cotswolds, features everything that is best about this region of Britain. The rivers, valleys and green rolling hills form an excellent backdrop for attractive stone villages, historic churches, country houses and a dose of ecclesiastical history. At Hinton Charterhouse, for example, the walk passes the remains of a 13th century priory. Unfortunately, this is on private land, but tantalising glimpses of the ancient landmark can be glimpsed through the trees.

Hills are an inevitable feature of any walk in the Bath area. Although this is no exception, the various uphill sections of the walk are short and staggered. You will be surprised to discover that between The Inn at Freshford and Hinton Charterhouse church, there is a 425 ft height difference!

The Walk

From The Inn, walk back uphill into Freshford village. At the top of the hill, alongside the rather plain church, the road bears to the left. In a short distance, where the road bears right, continue straight ahead along a quiet byway signposted to Sharpstone. The next section of road passes alongside a small green, where wooden seats, springtime daffodils and views to the north across Freshford and Limpley Stoke might easily detain you. Continue along this lane until you reach a war memorial, where you fork left and head into Sharpstone. This hamlet is a delightful mixture of traditional stone cottages and houses, situated high on the hillside above the Frome valley. You will shortly reach a T-junction in front of Abbotsleigh Coach House. Turn right, head up the hill for 200 yards to another junction, and turn left and follow Abbey Lane up to the busy A36. The first mile of the walk has been road walking, but along quiet village streets with much of architectural merit to detain the eye.

Turn right along the A36 for literally a few yards, and look out for a stile and footpath sign on the opposite side of the road. Cross the main road with care, and beyond the stile bear left across the open field, looking out for a stile in the fence 50 yards beyond a house. Head straight across the next two fields, making for the stiles in the far hedgerows in both cases, to a third larger field. In this field, cross to the far hedgerow, bearing slightly to the right, where one final stile brings you out onto the Hinton Charterhouse road. Incidentally, during this section of field walking, you will have passed the remains of Hinton Priory beyond the hedgerow on your left-hand side. This Carthusian priory was founded in 1232 and abandoned at the Dissolution of the Monasteries some three centuries later.

Cross the Hinton road, and follow the footpath signposted into the field opposite. Bear slightly to the right across the field ahead, making for the prominent Hinton church on the crest of the hill. The stile that leads into the churchyard is alongside the trees to the left of the church. I could find no reference to the church in any local guides, which probably does this fine building a great disservice! In its favour, the seat in the churchyard does provide an excellent resting place at the half-way point on the walk.

Outside the church, turn left along the road. Continue past the Old School out of the village, ignore the subsequent right-turn signposted to Trowbridge, and continue on to the A36. Cross this main road, and follow the cul-de-sac lane opposite down through Friary Wood to a small hamlet known simply as Friary. This was the site of quarters for the lay brothers from Hinton Priory. When you reach the first cottage, cross the stream on your left and climb the pasture up to a gate in the corner. Follow the enclosed path beyond the gate back towards Sharpstone and Freshford. This path provides an excellent vantage point as it passes across the hillside above the Frome. All too soon, the path ends in front of Middle House, where you turn right out onto the Freshford road. Turn right, follow the road alongside and over the Frome, and continue around to the front of the factory complex housed in old Freshford Mill. This was another property that originally belonged to Hinton Priory. After the dissolution, it functioned as a cloth and flock mill, and has more recently been a part of the local rubber industry.

In front of the factory complex, you will find a footpath signposted on the left-hand side. The path leads across a couple of fields to join the Westwood to Freshford road. The bridge alongside The Inn at Freshford is a landmark to aim for. Join the road, and turn left to walk the few yards back to The Inn. It is worth pausing as you cross the Frome to see if you can spot the trout in its sparkling waters. This is a sure sign of that rarity nowadays – a clean, unpolluted waterway.

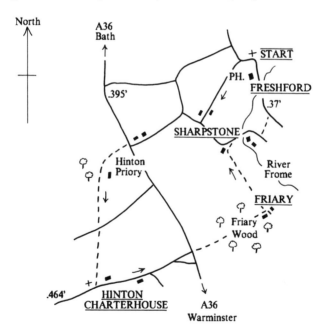

Not to scale.

127